CABLE Couture

BY KNIT PICKS

Copyright © 2018 Knit Picks

All rights reserved. This book or any portion thereof may not be reproduced or used in any manner whatsoever without the express written permission of the publisher except for the use of brief quotations in a book review.

Photography by Amy Setter

Printed in the United States of America

First Printing, 2018

ISBN 978-1-62767-205-4

Versa Press, Inc

800-447-7829

www.versapress.com

CONTENTS

Allotrope Sweater	5
Cable Car Pullover	17
Corrie Sweater	23
Game Theory	31
Havana	39
Passage Cardigan	45
Plait Pullover	51
Tweedy Jumper	59
Woodstock	67

ALLOTROPE SWEATER

by Lynnette Hulse

FINISHED MEASUREMENTS
33.5 (36.75, 41, 46.25, 50.5, 55.75)" finished bust measurement; garment is meant to be worn with approximately 4" of positive ease.

YARN
Knit Picks Stroll Sock Yarn
(75% Fine Superwash Merino Wool, 25% Nylon; 231 yards/50g): MC Dove Heather 25023, 3 (3, 4, 4, 5, 5) balls; C1 Jack Rabbit Heather 25610 2 (3, 3, 3, 4, 4) balls; C2 Grizzly Heather 27238, C3 Fedora 25030, 2 (2, 3, 3, 4, 4) balls each.

NEEDLES
US 6 (4mm) circular needles, or 2 sizes smaller than size to obtain gauge.

US 8 (5mm) circular needles, or size to obtain gauge.

NOTIONS
Yarn Needle
Lockable Stitch Markers
Cable Needle
Scrap Yarn or Stitch Holders

GAUGE
20 sts and 40 rows = 4" in 1x1 Rib in the rnd on smaller needles with yarn held double, blocked.

15 sts and 24 rows = 4" in Reverse St st in the rnd on larger needles with yarn held double, blocked.

27 sts and 26 rows = 4" over 33.5-41" Allotrope Twist Chart on larger needles with yarn held double, blocked.

21 sts and 26 rows = 4" over 46.25-55.75" Allotrope Twist Chart rep section on larger needles with yarn held double, blocked.

4 sts and 6 rows = 1" over four stitch cable on larger needles with yarn held double, blocked.

(Gauge for this project is approximate)

For pattern support, contact
nett@vintagenettles.net

Notes:

A wide, repeating diamond cable and a four-color fade feature in Allotrope. Knit top down, this loose raglan sweater is worked seamlessly in reverse stockinette with a split hem and extra-long sleeves. The pattern's bold and impressive, yet easy-to-knit cables shine in both the solid and color transitions. Sock yarn held double in alternating marled combinations subtly blend one color to the next in reverse stockinette.

When working a chart in the rnd, read each row from right to left, as a RS row.

Allotrope Twist Chart Pattern for sizes 33.5, 36.75, 41" (in the rnd over an even number of sts)
Rnd 1: K3, P4, 3/3 LC, P8, 3/3 LC, P4, K3. 34 sts.
Rnd 2: K3, P4, K6, P8, K6, P4, K3.
Rnd 3: K3, P2, 3/2 RPC, 3/2 LPC, P4, 3/2 RPC, 3/2 LPC, P2, K3.
Rnd 4: K3, P2, (K3, P4) x 3, K3, P2, K3.
Rnd 5: K3, (3/2 RPC, P4, 3/2 LPC) x 2, K3.
Rnd 6: (K6, P8) x 2, K6.
Rnd 7: (3/3 LC, P8) x 2, 3/3 LC.
Rnds 8 - 10: (K6, P8) x 2, K6.
Rnd 11: Rep Rnd 7.
Rnd 12: Rep Rnd 6.
Rnd 13: K3, (3/2 LPC, P4, 3/2 RPC) x 2, K3.
Rnd 14: Rep Rnd 4.
Rnd 15: K3, P2, 3/2 LPC, 3/2 RPC, P4, 3/2 LPC, 3/2 RPC, P2, K3.
Rnd 16: Rep Rnd 2.
Rnd 17: Rep Rnd 1.
Rnds 18 - 20: K3, P4, K6, P8, K6, P4, K3.
Rep Rnds 1-20 for pattern.

Allotrope Twist Chart Pattern for sizes 46.25, 50.5, 55.75" (in the rnd over an even number of sts)
Work Rnds 1-36, then cont to rep Rnds 17-36 to Front Hem Split separation.
Rnd 1: K3, P4, 3/3 LC, P8, 3/3 LC, P4, K3. 34 sts.
Rnd 2: K3, P4, K6, P8, K6, P4, K3.
Rnd 3: K3, P2, 3/2 RPC, 3/2 LPC, P4, 3/2 RPC, 3/2 LPC, P2, K3.
Rnd 4: K3, P2, (K3, P4) x 3, K3, P2, K3.
Rnd 5: K3, (3/2 RPC, P4, 3/2 LPC) x 2, K3.
Rnd 6: (K6, P8) x 2, K6.
Rnd 7: (3/3 LC, P8) x 2, 3/3 LC.
Rnds 8 - 10: (K6, P8) x 2, K6.
Rnd 11: Rep Rnd 7.
Rnd 12: Rep Rnd 6.
Rnd 13: Remove M, move M back 2 sts, (3/2 RPC, 3/2 LPC, P4) x 2, 3/2 RPC, 3/2 LPC. 38 sts.
Rnd 14: (K3, P4) x 5, K3.
Rnd 15: Remove M, move M back 2 sts, (3/2 RPC, P4, 3/2 LPC) x 3. 42 sts.
Rnd 16: K3, (P8, K6) x 2, P8, K3.
Rnd 17: Remove M, move M back 2 sts, ((3/3 LC, P8) x 3, 3/3 LC). 48 sts.
Rnds 18 - 20: ((K6, P8) x 3, K6).
Rnd 21: Rep Rnd 17.
Rnd 22: (K3, P11, K6, P8, K6, P11, K3).
Rnd 23: (K3, (3/2 LPC, P4, 3/2 RPC) x 3, K3).
Rnd 24: (K3, P3, K2, (P4, K3) x 4, P4, K2, P3, K3).
Rnd 25: (K3, P2, (3/2 LPC, 3/2 RPC, P4) x 2, 3/2 LPC, 3/2 RPC, P2, K3).
Rnd 26: (K3, P4, (K6, P8) x 2, K6, P4, K3).
Rnd 27: (K3, P4, (3/3 LC, P8) x 2, 3/3 LC, P4, K3).
Rnds 28 - 30: (K3, P4, (K6, P8) x 2, K6, P4, K3).
Rnd 31: Rep Rnd 27.
Rnd 32: Rep Rnd 26.
Rnd 33: (K3, P2, (3/2 RPC, 3/2 LPC, P4) x 2, 3/2 RPC, 3/2 LPC, P2, K3).
Rnd 34: (K3, P2, (K3, P4) x 5, K3, P2, K3).
Rnd 35: (K3, (3/2 RPC, P4, 3/2 LPC) x 3, K3).
Rnd 36: Rep Rnd 18.
Rep Rnds 17-36 for pattern, to Hem Split.

1/1 RPC: SL1 to CN, hold in back, P1, P1 from CN.
2/2 RC: SL2 to CN, hold in back, K2, K2 from CN.
3/2 LPC: SL3 to CN, hold in front, P2, K3 from CN.
3/2 RPC: SL2 to CN, hold in back, K3, P2 from CN.
3/3 LC: SL3 to CN, hold in front, K3, K3 from CN.
M1: Use a Backwards Loop CO. 1 st inc.

DS: Double Stitch, or German Short Row
Purl Side (RS): Turn work, and WYIF, SL1 st P-wise, then pull the yarn over to the back until it shows two legs on the needle and to be in position for the next knit st.
Knit Side (WS): Turn work, and WYIF, SL1 st P-wise, then pull the yarn over to the back until it shows two legs on the needle, then continue pulling the yarn over to the front to be ready to work the next purl st.

Alternate Cable Cast On
Make a slipknot and place on LH needle. K one st in knot, SL this new st K-wise to LH needle. *Make a P st: bring the yarn to the front, insert the working needle from back to front between first two sts on left needle. Wrap yarn as if to purl. Draw yarn through to back, and SL this new st K-wise to the LH needle. Make a K st: insert the working right needle from front to back between first two sts on left needle. Wrap yarn as if to K, and draw yarn back through to front, SL this new st K-wise to the LH needle. Rep from *.

Sewn K1, P1 Bind-off
Set Up, when working flat: With tail of yarn approximately three times the length needing to be BO, thread yarn needle. Insert needle P-wise into the first knit st, leave st on LH needle. Bring yarn needle to the back and pass through the 1st purl st K-wise, leaving this st on the needle. Set up edge complete – this can be omitted for binding off in the rnd.
Bind Off Repeat: WYIF, insert needle through first st K-wise, then SL st off the needle. Skip next purl st, and insert needle through next knit st on LH needle P-wise. Leave sts on needle. Bring yarn needle to back, insert needle through first purl st P-wise, and SL st off the left needle. Skip knit st, and insert needle through next purl st K-wise. Leave sts on needle. Rep until all sts have been BO.

DIRECTIONS

Collar
With MC held double and smaller needles, Alternate Cable Cast On 104 (108, 108, 108, 108, 112) sts.
Row 1: (K1, P1) to end. PM for beginning of rnd.
Join to work in the rnd, being careful not to twist sts.
Rnds 2 -7: (K1, P1) around.

Yoke
Set Up and Short Row Shaping
Change to larger needles.

Sizes 33.5, 36.75" Only

Rnd 1: P21(29, -, -, -, -) for Back, PM, K4 for Raglan Cable, PM, P19(17, -, -, -, -) Sleeve sts, PM, K4 for Raglan Cable, PM, K3, P2, K6, P7, K6, P2, K3 for Front, PM, K4 for Raglan Cable, PM, P19(17, -, -, -, -) Sleeve sts, PM, K4 for Raglan Cable. 7 markers placed, 8 total.
Row 2: M1, P to M, M1, SM, K4, SM, M1, P1, DS, K to M, SM, P4, SM, K to beginning of rnd, SM, P4, SM, M1, K1, DS, P to M, SM, K4, SM. 4 sts inc.
Row 3: M1, P to M, M1, SM, K4, SM, M1, P to 1 st after DS, DS, K to M, SM, P4, SM, K to beginning of rnd, SM, P4, SM, M1, K to 1 st after DS, DS, P to M, SM, K4, SM. 4 sts inc.
Row 4: Rep Row 3. 116, (120, -, -, -, -) sts on needles.
Rnd 5: P17(17, -, -, -, -), P2tog, (P to M, SM, 2/2 RC, SM) twice, K3, M1, P2, M1, K6, M1, P3, P2tog, P2, M1, K6, M1, P2, M1, K3, SM, 2/2 RC, SM, P to M, SM, 2/2 RC, SM. 120 (124, -, -, -, -) sts on needles. 120 (124, -, -, -, -) sts.
Rnd 6: M1, (P to M, M1, SM, K4, SM, M1) twice, PM, work Allotrope Twist Chart for desired size, M1, SM, K4, SM, M1, P to M, M1, SM, K4. 1 marker placed, 9 total. 128 (132, -, -, -, -) sts.

Sizes 41, 46.25, 50.5, 55.75" Only

Rnd 1: P-(-, 31, 33, 35, 37) for Back, PM, K4 for Raglan Cable, PM, P-(-, 15, 13, 11, 11) Sleeve sts, PM, K4 for Raglan Cable, PM, P-(-, 1, 2, 3, 4) for left Front, PM, K3, P2, K6, P7, K6, P2, K3, P-(-, 1, 2, 3, 4) for mid and right Front, PM, K4 for Raglan Cable, PM, P-(-, 15, 13, 11, 11) Sleeve sts, PM, K4 for Raglan Cable. 8 markers place, 9 total.
Row 2: M1, P to M, M1, SM, K4, SM, M1, P1, DS, K to M, SM, P4, SM, K to beginning of rnd, SM, P4, SM, M1, K1, DS, P to M, SM, K4, SM. 4 sts inc.
Row 3: M1, P to M, M1, SM, K4, SM, M1, P to 1 st after DS, DS, K to M, SM, P4, SM, K to beginning of rnd, SM, P4, SM, M1, K1 to 1 st after DS, DS, P to M, SM, K4, SM. 4 sts inc.
Row 4: Rep Row 3. -(-, 120, 120, 120, 124) sts on needles.
Rnd 5: P-(-, 17, 17, 17, 18), P2tog, (P to M, SM, 2/2 RC, SM) twice, P to M, SM, K3, M1, P2, M1, K6, M1, P3, P2tog, P2, M1, K6, M1, P2, M1, K3, (P to M, SM, 2/2 RC, SM) twice. -(-, 124, 124, 124, 128) sts on needles.
Rnd 6: M1 (P to M, M1, SM, K4, SM, M1) twice, P to M, SM, work Allotrope Twist Chart for desired size, P to M, SM, K4, SM, M1, P to M, M1, SM, K4. -(-, 132, 132, 132, 136) sts on needles.

All Sizes
Rnd 1: (P to M, SM, K4, SM) twice, P to M, SM, work Allotrope Twist Chart for desired size, (P to M, SM, K4, SM) twice.
Rnd 2: M1 (P to M, M1, SM, K4, SM, M1) twice, P to M, SM, work Allotrope Twist Chart for desired size, P to M, M1, SM, K4, SM, M1, P to M, M1, SM, K4, SM. 8 sts inc.
Rnds 3 – 4: Rep Rnds 1 – 2.
Rnd 5: (P to M, SM, 2/2 RC, SM) twice, P to M, M1, SM, work Allotrope Twist Chart, M1, (P to M, SM, 2/2 RC, SM) twice. 2 sts inc.
Rnd 6: Rep Rnd 2.
Rnds 7-10: Rep Rnds 1-2.
Rnd 11: Rep Rnd 5.
Rep Rnds 6 – 11 1 (1, 1, 2, 2, 2) times more. For Sizes 46.25, 50.5, 55.75", move M at beginning of Allotrope Twist Chart back 2 sts on chart Rnds 13, 15 and 3 sts on Rnd 17. 198 (202, 202, 228, 228, 232) sts on needles. 44 (52, 54, 62, 64, 66) sts in back and 58 (58, 60, 70, 72, 74) sts in front, 40 (38, 36, 40, 38, 38) sts for each sleeve, 16 sts total for 4 raglan shoulder cables.
Rnd 12: Rep Rnd 2.
Rnd 13: Rep Rnd 1.
Rnds 14 – 16: Cont to rep Rnd 2 then Rnd 1, ending with a Rnd 2 rep.
Rnd 17: (P to M, SM, 2/2 RC, SM) twice, P to M, SM, work Allotrope Twist Chart, (P to M, SM, 2/2 RC, SM) twice.
Rep Rnds 12-17 0 (0, 1, 1, 2, 3) times more. 222 (226, 250, 276, 300, 328) sts on needles. 50 (58, 66, 74, 82, 90) sts in back and 64 (64, 72, 82, 90, 98) sts in front, 46 (44, 48, 52, 56, 62) sts for each sleeve, 16 sts total for 4 raglan shoulder cables.

Sizes 36.75, 41, 46.25, 50.5" Only
Rnd 1: P to M, SM, K4, SM, M1, P to M, M1, SM, K4, SM, P to M, DM, work Allotrope Twist Chart, P to M, SM, K4, SM, M1, P to M, M1, SM, K4, SM. 4 sts inc, 2 in each Sleeve.
Rnd 2: (P to M, SM, K4, SM) twice, P to M, SM, work Allotrope Twist Chart, (P to M, SM, K4) twice.
Rnds 3 – 5: Rep Rnds 1 - 2, ending with a Rnd 1 rep. 8 sts inc.
Rnd 6: (P to M, SM, 2/2 RC, SM) twice, P to M, SM, work Allotrope Twist Chart, (P to M, SM, 2/2 RC, SM) twice. - (238, 262, 288, 312, -) sts, - (50, 54, 58, 62, -) sts for each sleeve.

Sizes 33.5, S, 41, 46.25, 55.75" Only
Rnds 1-5: (P to M, SM, K4, SM) twice, P to M, SM, work Allotrope Twist Chart, (P to M, SM, K4, SM) twice.
Rnd 6: (P to M, SM, 2/2 RC, SM) twice, P to M, SM, work Allotrope Twist Chart, (P to M, SM, 2/2 RC, SM) twice.
Rep Rnds 1 – 6 1 (0, 0, 0, -, 0) times more.

222 (238, 262, 288, 312, 328) sts on needles. 50 (58, 66, 74, 82, 90) sts in back and 64 (64, 72, 82, 90, 98) sts in front, 46 (50, 54, 58, 62, 62) sts for each sleeve, 16 sts total for 4 raglan shoulder cables.

Begin MC to MC+C1 Color Change
Drop one MC strand, and hold one strand MC and one strand C1 tog.
Rnd 1: (P to M, SM, K4, SM) twice, P to M, SM, work Allotrope Twist Chart, (P to M, SM, K4, SM) twice.
Drop C1 strand and resume holding two strands MC tog.
Rnd 2: (P to M, SM, K4, SM) twice, P to M, SM, work Allotrope Twist Chart, (P to M, SM, K4, SM) twice.
Rnd 3: Rep Rnd 2.
Rnds 4-5: Rep Rnds 1-2, changing yarns as directed.
Rnd 6: (P to M, SM, 2/2 RC, SM) twice, P to M, SM, work Allotrope Twist Chart, (P to M, SM, 2/2 RC, SM) twice.

Separate Body and Sleeves

With one strand MC and one strand C1; P to M, SM, K4, SM, Backwards Loop CO 6 (8, 8, 8, 8, 10) sts, place next 46 (50, 54, 58, 62, 62) sts on scrap yarn, SM, K4, SM, P to M, SM, work Allotrope Twist Chart, P to M, SM, K4, SM, Backwards Loop CO 6 (8, 8, 8, 8, 10) sts, place next 46 (50, 54, 58, 62, 62) on scrap yarn, K4, SM. 142 (154, 170, 188, 204, 224) sts on needles.

Body

Drop C1 strand, and hold two strands of MC tog.
Rnd 1: (P to M, SM, K4, SM) twice, P to M, SM, work Allotrope Twist Chart, (P to M, SM, K4, SM) twice.
Drop one MC strand, and hold one strand MC and one strand C1 tog.
Rnd 2: Rep Rnd 1.
Rnds 3-4: Rep Rnds 1-2, maintaining color changes.
Drop C1 strand, and hold two strands of MC tog.
Rnd 5: (P to M, SM, 2/2 RC, SM) twice, P to M, SM, work Allotrope Twist Chart, (P to M, SM, 2/2 RC, SM) twice.
Cut one strand of MC, leaving a 4" tail and hold one strand of MC and one strand of C1 tog for Rnds 6-11.
Rnds 6-10: Rep Rnd 1.
Rnd 11: Rep Rnd 5.

Begin MC+C1 to C1 Color Change

Drop MC strand, and hold two strands of C1 tog.
Rnd 1: (P to M, SM, K4, SM) twice, P to M, SM, work Allotrope Twist Chart, (P to M, SM, K4, SM) twice.
Drop one C1 strand, and hold one strand MC and one strand C1 tog.
Rnds 2-3: Rep Rnd 1.
Drop MC strand, and hold two strands of C1 tog.
Rnd 4: Rep Rnd 1.
Drop one C1 strand, and hold one strand MC and one strand C1 tog.
Rnd 5: Rep Rnd 1.
Rnd 6: (P to M, SM, 2/2 RC, SM) twice, P to M, SM, work Allotrope Twist Chart, (P to M, SM, 2/2 RC, SM) twice.
Hold two strands of C1 tog.
Rnd 7: Rep Rnd 1.
Drop one C1 strand, and hold one strand MC and one strand C1 tog.
Rnd 8: Rep Rnd 1.
Rnds 9-11: Rep Rnds 7-8, maintaining color changes and ending on a Rnd 7 rep.
Drop one C1 strand, and hold one strand MC and one strand C1 tog.
Rnd 12: Rep Rnd 6.
Cut remaining strand of MC, leaving a 4" tail and hold two strands of C1 tog.
Rnds 13-18: Rep Rnds 1-6.

Begin C1 to C1+C2 Color Change
Sizes 41, 46.25, 50.5, 55.75" Only

Drop one C1 strand, and hold one strand C1 and one strand C2 tog.
Rnd 1: (P to M, SM, K4, SM) twice, P to M, SM, work Allotrope Twist Chart, (P to M, SM, K4, SM) twice.
Hold two strands of C1 tog.
Rnds 2-3: Rep Rnd 1.
Rnds 4-5: Rep Rnds 1-2, maintaining color changes,
Rnd 6: (P to M, SM, 2/2 RC, SM) twice, P to M, SM, work Allotrope Twist Chart, (P to M, SM, 2/2 RC, SM) twice.

All Sizes

Drop one C1 strand, and hold one strand C1 and one strand C2 tog.
Rnd 1: (P to M, SM, K4, SM) twice, P to M, SM, work Allotrope Twist Chart, (P to M, SM, K4, SM) twice.
Hold two strands of C1 tog.
Rnd 2: Rep Rnd 1.
Rnds 3-5: Rep Rnds 1-2, maintaining color changes and ending on a Rnd 1 rep.
Hold two strands of C1 tog.
Rnd 6: (P to M, SM, 2/2 RC, SM) twice, P to M, SM, work Allotrope Twist Chart, (P to M, SM, 2/2 RC, SM) twice.
Cut one strand of C1, leaving a 4" tail and hold one strand of C1 and one strand of C2 tog.
Rnds 7-12: Rep Rnds 1-6.

Begin C1+C2 to C2 Color Change
Sizes 41, 46.25, 50.5, 55.75" Only

Hold two strands of C2 tog.
Rnd 1: (P to M, SM, K4, SM) twice, P to M, SM, work Allotrope Twist Chart, (P to M, SM, K4, SM) twice.
Drop one C2 strand, and hold one strand C1 and one strand C2 tog.
Rnds 2-3: Rep Rnd 1.
Rnds 4-5: Rep Rnds 1-2, maintaining color changes.
Rnd 6: (P to M, SM, 2/2 RC, SM) twice, P to M SM, work Allotrope Twist Chart, (P to M, SM, 2/2 RC, SM) twice.

All Sizes

Hold two strands of C2 tog.
Rnd 1: (P to M, SM, K4, SM) twice, P to M, SM, work Allotrope Twist Chart, (P to M, SM, K4, SM) twice.
Drop one C2 strand, and hold one strand C1 and one strand C2 tog.
Rnd 2: Rep Rnd 1.
Rnds 3-5: Rep Rnds 1-2, maintaining color changes and ending on a Rnd 1 rep.
Drop one C2 strand, and hold one strand C1 and one strand C2 tog.

Rnd 6: M1, P to M, M1, SM, 2/2 RC, SM, P to M, SM, 2/2 RC, SM, P2tog, P to M, SM, work Allotrope Twist Chart, P to 2 sts from M, P2tog, SM, 2/2 RC, SM, P to M, SM, 2/2 RC, SM. 2 sts inc on Back, 2 sts dec on Front.
Cut remaining strand of C1, leaving a 4" tail and hold two strands of C2 tog.
Rnds 7-12: Rep Rnds 1-6.

Begin C2 to C2+C3 Color Change
Sizes 50.5, 55.75" Only
Drop one C2 strand, and hold one strand C2 and one strand C3 tog.
Rnd 1: (P to M, SM, K4, SM) twice, P to M, SM, work Allotrope Twist Chart, (P to M, SM, K4, SM) twice.
Hold two strands of C2 tog.
Rnds 2-3: Rep Rnd 1.
Rnds 4-5: Rep Rnds 1-2, maintaining color changes,
Rnd 6: (P to M, SM, 2/2 RC, SM) twice, P to M, SM, work Allotrope Twist Chart, (P to M, SM, 2/2 RC, SM) twice.

All Sizes
Drop one C2 strand, and hold one strand C2 and one strand C3 tog.
Rnd 1: (P to M, SM, K4, SM) twice, P to M, SM, work Allotrope Twist Chart, (P to M, SM, K4, SM) twice.
Hold two strands of C2 tog.
Rnd 2: Rep Rnd 1.
Rnds 3-5: Rep Rnds 1-2, maintaining color changes and ending on a Rnd 1 rep.
Hold two strands of C2 tog.
Rnd 6: M1, P to M, M1, SM, 2/2 RC, SM, P to M, SM, 2/2 RC, SM, P2tog, P to M, SM, work Allotrope Twist Chart, P to 2 sts from M, P2tog, SM, 2/2 RC, SM, P to M, SM, 2/2 RC, SM. 2 sts inc on Back, 2 sts dec on Front.
Cut one strand of C2, leaving a 4" tail and hold one strand of C2 and one strand of C3 tog.
Rnds 7-12: Rep Rnds 1-6.

Begin C2+C3 to C3 Color Change
Sizes 50.5, 55.75" Only
Hold two strands of C3 tog.
Rnd 1: (P to M, SM, K4, SM) twice, P to M, SM, work Allotrope Twist Chart, (P to M, SM, K4, SM) twice.
Drop one C3 strand, and hold one strand C2 and one strand C3 tog.
Rnds 2-3: Rep Rnd 1.
Rnds 4-5: Rep Rnds 1-2, maintaining color changes.
Rnd 6: (P to M, SM, 2/2 RC, SM) twice, P to M, SM, work Allotrope Twist Chart, (P to M, SM, 2/2 RC, SM) twice.

All Sizes
Hold two strands of C3 tog.
Rnd 1: (P to M, SM, K4, SM) twice, P to M, SM, work Allotrope Twist Chart, (P to M, SM, K4, SM) twice.
Drop one C3 strand, and hold one strand C2 and one strand C3 tog.
Rnd 2: Rep Rnd 1.
Rnds 3-5: Rep Rnds 1-2, maintaining color changes and ending on a Rnd 1 rep.
Drop one C3 strand, and hold one strand C2 and one strand C3 tog.
Rnd 6: (P to M, SM, 2/2 RC, SM) twice, P to M, SM, work Allotrope Twist Chart, (P to M, SM, 2/2 RC, SM) twice.
Cut remaining strand of C2, leaving a 4" tail and hold two strands of C3 tog.
Rnds 7-12: Rep Rnds 1-6.

Separate for Front Split Hem
Rnd 1: P to M, SM, K4, SM, P2 (3, 3, 3, 3, 4), 1/1 RPC, P to M, SM, K4, P to M, SM, work Allotrope Twist Chart, P to M, SM, K4, SM, P2 (3, 3, 3, 3, 4), 1/1 RPC, P to M, SM, K4, SM.
Rnd 2: P to M, SM, K4, SM, P3 (4, 4, 4, 4, 5), (K1, P1) to fifth marker from start of ribbing, removing markers as you come to them, continue (K1, P1) for 3 (4, 4, 4, 4, 5) more sts. Turn.
Rows 3-11 Work back and forth across front in 1x1 Rib.
BO front ribbing using a sewn K1, P1 Bind Off.

Back Split Hem
Rejoin C3 held double to remaining back sts, starting with the last st not worked before turning to work Front Hem flat.
Row 1: (P to M, SM, K4, SM) twice, P to end, removing markers as you come to them.
Row 2: (P1, K1) to end.
Row 3-16: Work back and forth in 1x1 Rib.
BO back ribbing using a sewn K1, P1 Bind Off.

Sleeves (make 2 the same)
Place 46 (50, 54, 58, 62, 62) sts from scrap yarn onto working needle. Hold one strand MC and one strand C1 tog. PU and K 3 (4, 4, 4, 4, 5) sts from the body at the underarm, PM for beginning of rnd, PU and K another 3 (4, 4, 4, 4, 5) sts from the body at the underarm and join to work in the rnd. 52 (58, 62, 66, 70, 72) sts.
Drop C1 strand, and hold two strands of MC tog.
Rnd 1: P all sts.
Drop one MC strand, and hold one strand MC and one strand C1 tog.
Rnd 2: P all sts.
Rnds 3-6: Rep Rnds 1-2 maintaining color changes.
Rnds 7-12: P all sts.

Begin MC+C1 to C1 Color Change
Drop MC strand, and hold two strands of C1 tog.
Rnd 1: P all sts.
Drop one C1 strand, and hold one strand of MC and one strand of C1 tog.
Rnds 2-3: P all sts.
Rnds 4-6: Rep Rnds 1-3, maintaining color changes.
Drop MC strand, and hold two strands of C1 tog.
Rnd 7: P all sts.
Drop one C1 strand, and hold one strand of MC and one strand of C1 tog.

Rnd 8: P all sts.
Rnds 9-12: Rep Rnds 7-8, maintaining color changes.
Drop MC strand, and hold two strands of C1 tog.
Rnds 13-18: P all sts.

Begin C1 to C1+C2 Color Change

Drop one strand of C1, and hold one strand of C1 and one strand of C2 tog.
Rnd 1: P all sts.
Drop C2 strand, and hold two strands of C1 tog.
Rnds 2-3: P all sts.
Drop one C2 strand, and hold one strand of C1 and one strand of C2 tog.
Rnd 4: P all sts.
Drop C2 strand, and hold two strands of C1 tog.
Rnds 5-6: P all sts.
Drop one C1 strand, and hold one strand of C1 and one strand of C2 tog.
Rnd 7: P1, P0(0, 2, 2, 2, 2)tog, P to 3 sts from end, P0(0, 2, 2, 2, 2)tog, P to end. 52 (58, 60, 64, 68, 70) sts.
Drop C2 strand, and hold two strands of C1 tog.
Rnd 8: P all sts.
Drop one C1 strand, and hold one strand of C1 and one strand of C2 tog.
Rnd 9: P all sts
Rnds 10-12: Rep Rnds 8-9, maintaining color changes, ending with a Rnd 8 rep.
Drop one C1 strand, and hold one strand of C1 and one strand of C2 tog.
Rnd 13: P1, P2(2, 0, 0, 2, 2)tog, P to 3 sts from end, P2(2, 0, 0, 2, 2)tog, P to end. 50 (56, 60, 64, 66, 68) sts.

Rnds 14-18: P all sts.

Begin C1+C2 to C2 Color Change

Drop C1 strand, and hold two strands of C2 tog.
Rnd 1: P1, P0(0, 2, 2, 2, 2)tog, P to 3 sts from end, P0(0, 2, 2, 2, 2)tog, P to end. 50 (56, 58, 62, 64, 66) sts.
Drop one C2 strand, and hold one strand of C1 and one strand of C2 tog.
Rnds 2-3: P all sts.
Drop C1 strand, and hold two strands of C2 tog.
Rnd 4: P all sts.
Drop one C2 strand, and hold one strand of C1 and one strand of C2 tog.
Rnds 5-6: P all sts.
Drop C1 strand, and hold two strands of C2 tog.
Rnd 7: P1, P2tog, P to 3 sts from end, P2tog, P1. 48 (54, 56, 60, 62, 64) sts.
Drop one C2 strand, and hold one strand of C1 and one strand of C2 tog.
Rnd 8: P all sts.
Drop C1 strand, and hold two strands of C2 tog.
Rnd 9: P all sts
Rnds 10-12: Rep Rnds 8-9, maintaining color changes, ending with a Rnd 8 rep.
Drop C1 strand, and hold two strands of C2 tog.
Rnd 13: P1, P0(2, 2, 2, 2, 2)tog, P to 3 sts from end, P0(2, 2, 2, 2, 2)tog, P to end. 48 (52, 54, 58, 60, 62) sts.
Rnds 14-18: P all sts.

Begin C2 to C2+C3 Color Change

Drop one strand C2, and hold one strand of C2 and one strand of C3 tog.

Rnd 1: P1, P2tog, P to 3 sts from end, P2tog, P1. 46 (50, 52, 56, 58, 60) sts.
Drop C3 strand, and hold two strands of C2 tog.
Rnds 2-3: P all sts.
Drop one C2 strand, and hold one strand of C2 and one strand of C3 tog.
Rnd 4: P all sts.
Drop C3 strand, and hold two strands of C2 tog.
Rnds 5-6: P all sts.
Drop one C2 strand, and hold one strand of C2 and one strand of C3 tog.
Rnd 7: P1, P0(2, 2, 2, 2, 2)tog, P to 3 sts from end, P0(2, 2, 2, 2, 2)tog, P to end. 46 (48, 50, 54, 56, 58) sts.
Drop C3 strand, and hold two strands of C2 tog.
Rnd 8: P all sts.
Drop one C2 strand, and hold one strand of C2 and one strand of C3 tog.
Rnd 9: P all sts
Rnds 10-12: Rep Rnds 8-9, maintaining color changes, ending with a Rnd 8 rep.
Drop one C2 strand, and hold one strand of C2 and one strand of C3 tog.
Rnd 13: P1, P2tog, P to 3 sts from end, P2tog, P1. 44 (46, 48, 52, 54, 56) sts.
Rnds 14-18: P all sts.

Begin C2+C3 to C3 Color Change
Drop C2 strand, and hold two strands of C3 tog.
Rnd 1: P1, P2tog, P to 3 sts from end, P2tog, P1. 42 (44, 46, 50 52, 54) sts.

Drop one C3 strand, and hold one strand of C2 and one strand of C3 tog.
Rnds 2-3: P all sts.
Drop C2 strand, and hold two strands of C3 tog.
Rnd 4: P all sts.
Drop one C3 strand, and hold one strand of C2 and one strand of C3 tog.
Rnds 5-6: P all sts.
Drop C2 strand, and hold two strands of C3 tog.
Rnd 7: P1, P2tog, P to 3 sts from end, P2tog, P1. 40 (42, 44, 48, 50, 52) sts.
Drop one C3 strand, and hold one strand of C2 and one strand of C3 tog.
Rnd 8: P all sts.
Drop C2 strand, and hold two strands of C3 tog.
Rnd 9: P all sts
Rnds 10-12: Rep Rnds 8-9, maintaining color changes, ending with a Rnd 8 rep.
Drop C2 strand, and hold two strands of C3 tog.
Rnd 13-24: P all sts.

Sizes 46.25, 50.5, 55.75" Only: P 6 rnds in C3.

Ribbed Cuff
Switch to smaller needles.
Rnds 1-11: Work in (K1, P1) rib.
BO using a sewn K1, P1 Bind Off.

Finishing
Weave in ends, wash and block to diagram.

A 20.75 (21.5, 21.5, 21.5, 21.5, 22.5)"
B 13.75 (15.5, 16.5, 17.5, 18.75, 19.25)"
C 10.75 (11.25, 11.75, 12.75, 13.25, 13.75)"
D 20.75 (20.75, 20.75, 21.75, 21.75, 21.75)"
E 33.5 (36.75, 43, 46.25, 50.5, 55.75)"
F 14 (14, 14, 16, 16, 18, 18)"
G 8 (8, 9, 9.75, 9.75, 10.75)"

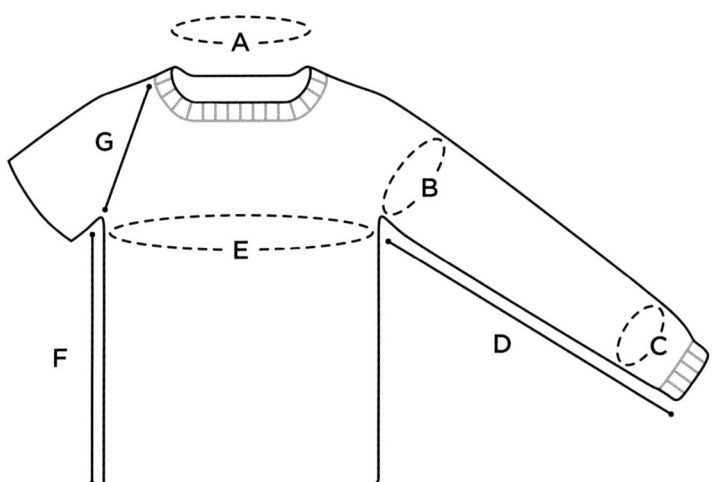

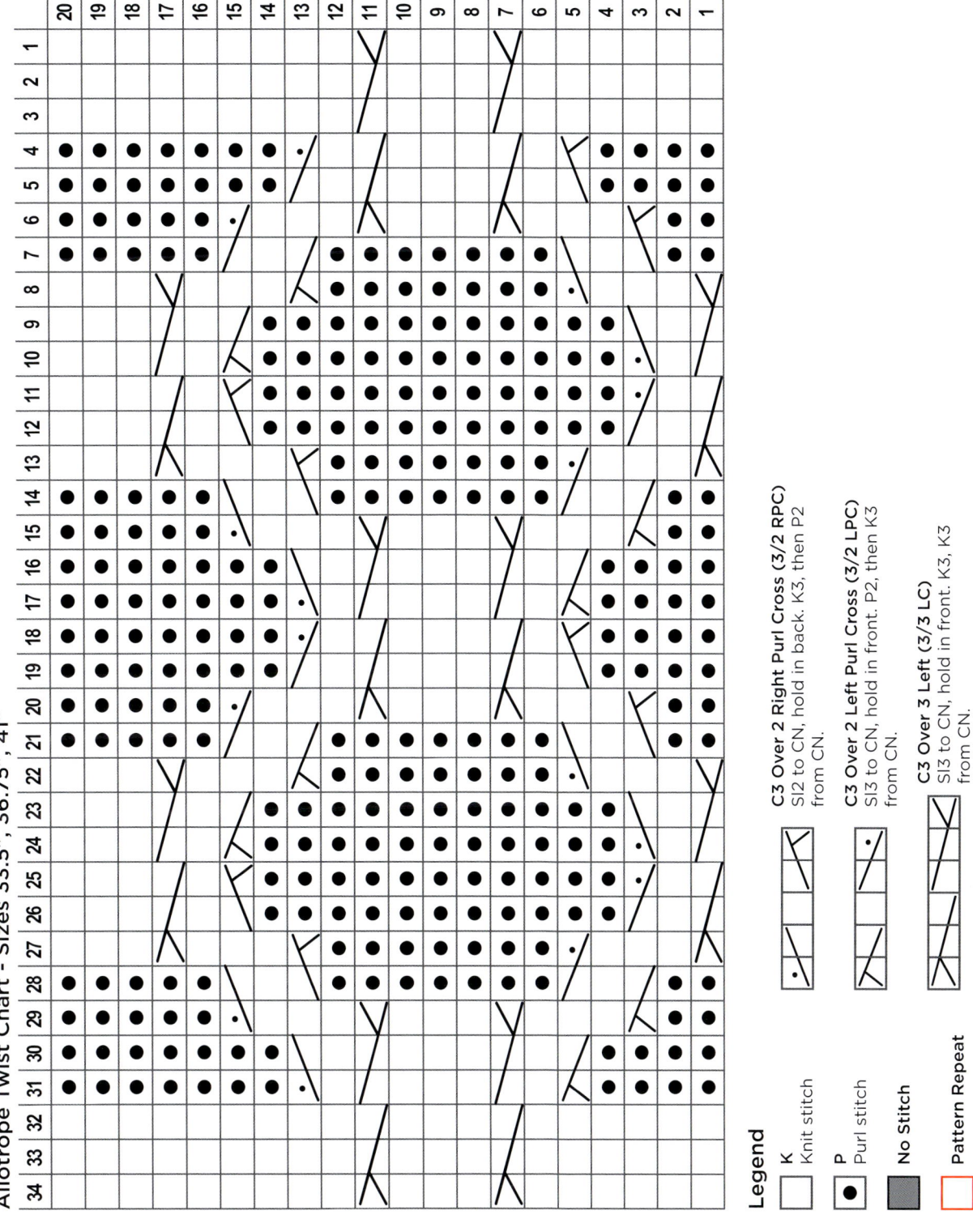

Allotrope Twist Chart - Sizes 46.25", 50.5", 55.75"

CABLE CAR PULLOVER

by Donna Estin

FINISHED MEASUREMENTS
36 (40, 44, 48.75, 52.75)" finished bust measurement; garment is meant to be worn with 4" of positive ease.

YARN
Knit Picks Swish Worsted
(100% Fine Superwash Merino Wool; 110 yards/50g): Delft Heather 24095, 11 (12, 14, 15, 17) balls.

NEEDLES
US 6 (4mm) 16" circular needles plus straight or circular needles, or one size smaller than size to obtain gauge.

US 7 (4.5mm) 16" circular needles plus straight or circular needles, or size to obtain gauge.

NOTIONS
Yarn Needle
Stitch Markers
Cable Needle

GAUGE
20 sts and 26 rows = 4" in St st, blocked

26 sts = 4" over Cable Car chart, blocked.

20 sts and 26 rows = 4" in 1x2 Ribbing, slightly stretched and blocked.

For pattern support, contact donnaestindesigns@gmail.com

Notes:
Dramatic cables intertwine with each other to define this loose-fitting pullover, separating the two patterns along a diagonal incline.

The Cable Car Pullover is worked flat from the bottom up. When blocking the front and back, stretch out ribbing approximately 2" wider than schematic and let it dry flat. It will draw in a bit once dry. Allow the sleeve cuff and neck ribbing to dry without stretching.

When working the chart, follow RS rows (odd numbers) from right to left, and WS rows (even numbers) from left to right.

1x2 Ribbing (worked flat over a multiple of 3 sts)
Row 1 (RS): *P2, K1; rep from * to end.
Row 2 (WS): *P1, K2; rep from * to end.
Rep Rows 1-2 for pattern.

Cable Car Pattern (worked flat over 13 sts)
Row 1 (RS): P2, K2, P4, K4, P1.
Row 2 (WS): K1, P4, K4, P2, K2.
Row 3: P2, 2/2 LPC, P2, K4, P1.
Row 4: K1, P4, K2, P2, K4.
Row 5: P4, 2/2 LC, 2/2 LPC, P1.
Row 6: K1, P2, K2, P4, K4.
Row 7: P2, 2/2 RPC, 2/2 LPC, K2, P1.
Row 8: K1, P4, K4, P2, K2.
Row 9: P2, K2, P4, 2/2 LC, P1.
Row 10: Rep Row 8.
Rep Rows 3-10 for pattern.

2/2 LC: Sl 2 sts to CN and hold in front, K2, K2 from CN.
2/2 LPC: Sl 2 sts to CN and hold in front, P2, K2 from CN.
2/2 RPC: Sl 2 sts to CN and hold in back, K2, P2 from CN.

DIRECTIONS

Back
With larger needles, CO 95 (105, 115, 127, 137) sts.
Begin Hem (RS): K 21 (25, 32, 38, 42) sts, PM, work Row 1 of Cable Chart or line-by-line Cable Car Pattern over 13 sts, PM, work Row 1 of 1x2 Ribbing to last st, K1.
Next Row (WS): P1, work Row 2 of 1x2 Ribbing to M, SM, work Row 2 of Cable Chart, SM, P to end.

Body
All RS Rows: Work in St st (K on RS, P on WS) until last st before M, KFB, SM, work next row of Cable Chart, SM, P2tog, work in 1x2 Ribbing to last st, K1.
All WS Rows: K all K sts, P all P sts, cont working next WS row of chart as established.
Cont to work in established pattern, inc 1 and dec 1 st every RS row, until piece measures 15.5 (16, 16.5, 17, 17.5)", end with RS row.

Armholes
Next Row (WS): Purl, dec 3 sts evenly between M, purl to end. 92 (102, 112, 124, 134) sts. Work rest of back in St st, without inc or dec.
Shape Armholes: Beginning with next row (RS), BO 5 (5, 6, 6, 6) sts at beginning of next 2 rows, then 2 (2, 3, 3, 5) sts at beginning of next 2 rows. 78 (88, 94, 106, 112) sts.

Dec Row (RS): K1, SSK, K to last 3 sts, K2tog, K1. 2 sts dec. Rep Dec Row every RS row 2 (4, 5, 8, 10) more times. 72 (78, 82, 88, 90) sts.

Cont to work in St st until armhole measures 8 (8.5, 9, 9.5, 10)", end with a WS row. Note: Measure vertically, while letting weight of piece hang from needles.

Divide for Neck

Next Row (RS): K20 (22, 23, 26, 26) sts, join 2nd ball, BO center 32 (34, 36, 36, 38) sts, K to end. Working both sides at the same time, P next row.

Shape Shoulders

Next Row (RS): BO 10 (11, 11, 13, 13) sts, K to last 3 sts on right shoulder, K2tog, K1. 9 (10, 11, 12, 12) right shoulder sts. With 2nd ball K1, SSK, K to end. 19 (21, 22, 25, 25) left shoulder sts. BO 10 (11, 11, 13, 13) left shoulder sts at beginning of next (WS) row, P right shoulder sts.

Beginning with a RS row, BO remaining 9 (10, 11, 12, 12) sts at beginning of next 2 rows.

Front

Work same as Back until armhole measures 5.5 (6, 6.5, 7, 7.5)", end with a WS row. 72 (78, 82, 88, 90) sts.

Divide for Neck

Next Row (RS): K29 (32, 33, 36, 37) sts, join 2nd ball, BO center 14 (14, 16, 16, 16) sts, K to end. Working both sides at the same time, P next row.

Beginning with a RS row, BO 4 sts at beginning of each neck edge once, then 2 (3, 3, 3, 4) sts at beginning of each neck edge once, then 2 sts at beginning of each neck edge once. 21 (23, 24, 27, 27) sts per shoulder.

Dec Row (RS): K to last 2 sts on left shoulder, K2tog, K1. With 2nd ball, Sl1, SSK, K to end. 1 st dec each shoulder. Rep Dec Row once on next RS row. 19 (21, 22, 25, 25) sts per shoulder.

WE until armhole measures 8 (8.5, 9, 9.5, 10)", or same as Back, end with a WS row.

Shape Shoulders

Beginning with a RS row, BO 10 (11, 11, 13, 13) sts at beginning of next 2 rows, then BO 9 (10, 11, 12, 12) sts at beginning of next 2 rows.

Sleeves (make 2)

With larger needles CO 47 (50, 53, 53, 59) sts.
Beginning with a RS row, K1, work in 1x2 Ribbing to last st, K1. Maintaining first and last st of every row in St st for selvedges, work in 1x2 Ribbing for 3.5".
Change to smaller needles and cont as established until cuff measures 7" from CO, end with a RS row and dec 1 (0, 1, 1, 1) st on last row. 46 (50, 52, 52, 58) sts.

Next Row (WS of Cuff, RS of Sleeve): Change to larger needles and beginning with a K row, work in St st for 1.5", end with a WS row. Inc 1 st at each end of every 6th row 4 (2, 6, 14, 14) times and every following 8th row 7 (9, 6, 0, 0) times. 68 (72, 76, 80, 86) sts. When sleeve measures 21.5 (22, 22, 22.5, 22.5)", end with a WS row.

Shape Cap
Beginning with next row (RS), BO 5 (5, 6, 6, 6) sts at beginning of next 2 rows, then 2 (2, 3, 3, 5) sts at beginning of next 2 rows. 54 (58, 58, 62, 64) sts.

Dec Row (RS): K1, SSK, K to last 3 sts, K2tog, K1. 2 sts dec. Rep Dec Row every RS row 11 (13, 14, 15, 14) more times, then every other RS row 0 (0, 1, 1, 2) times. 30 (30, 26, 28, 30) sts. BO 2 sts at beginning of next 4 (4, 2, 2, 2) rows, then 3 sts at beginning of next 2 rows.
BO remaining 16 (16, 16, 18, 20) sts.

Finishing
Block pieces to schematic, refer to Notes for Ribbing. Sew shoulder seam. Set in sleeves and sew. For sleeve seam, begin seaming at cuff and place seam on WS of cuff so it can be folded back, then insert needle through fabric, flip sleeve over and continue seaming, placing seam on WS of sleeve. Fold cuff and sew in place (if desired). Sew side seams.

Neck
With smaller circular needles and RS facing, begin at left shoulder and PU 87 (90, 93, 96, 99) sts evenly around, join in the rnd, PM, careful not to twist.
Rnd 1: *K2, P1; rep from * to end.
Rep until neck measures 4". Change to larger circular needles and cont as established until neck measures 8". Loosely BO all sts in pattern. Fold over. Weave in yarn ends. Block neck, without stretching ribbing.

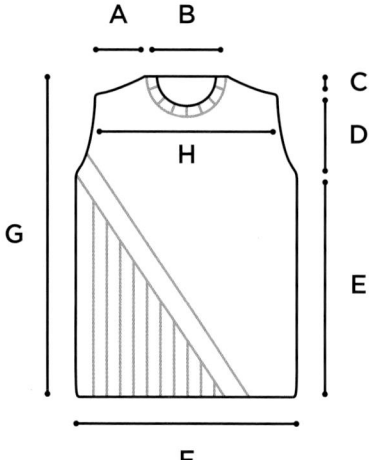 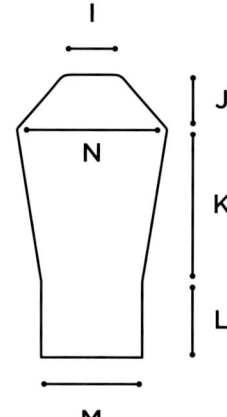

A 3.5 (4, 4.25, 4.75, 4.75)"
B 6.75 (7, 7.5, 7.5, 8)"
C 1"
D 8 (8.5, 9, 9.5, 10)"
E 15.5 (16, 16.5, 17, 17.5)"
F 18 (20, 22, 24.5, 26.5)"
G 24.5 (25.5, 26.5, 27.5, 28.5)"

H 14 (15.25, 16, 17.25, 17.5)"
I 3.25 (3.25, 3.25, 3.5, 4)"
J 5.25 (5.75, 6.5, 6.75, 7)"
K 14.5 (15, 15, 15.5, 15.5)"
L 7"
M 9 (9.5, 10.25, 10.25, 11.5)"
N 13.25 (14, 14.75, 15.5, 16.75)"

Note: Widths do not include selvedge stitches for seaming.

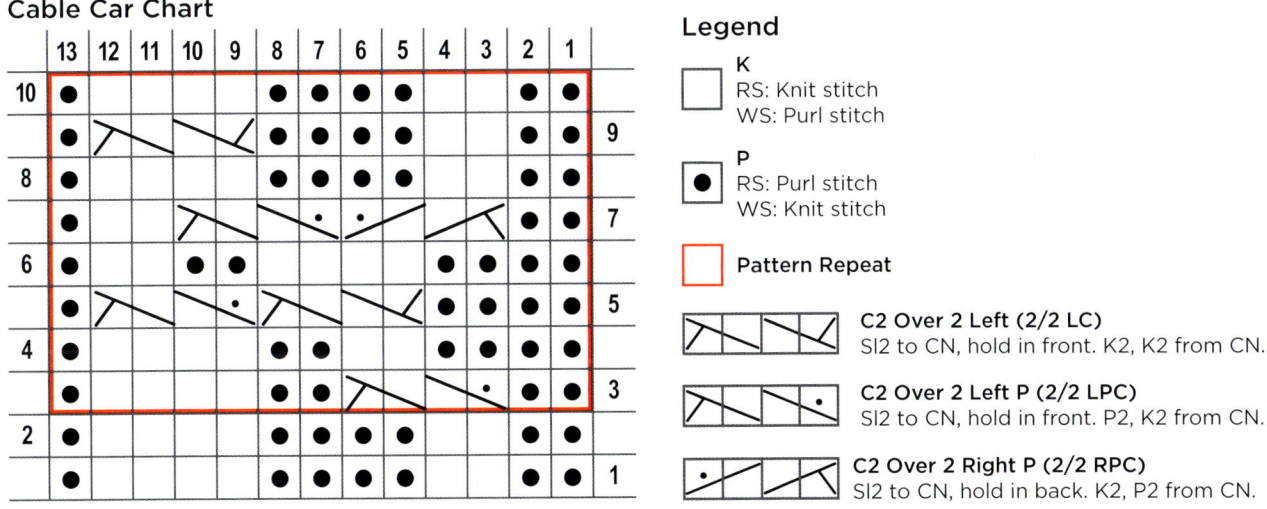

Cable Car Chart

Legend

- **K** — RS: Knit stitch / WS: Purl stitch
- **P** — RS: Purl stitch / WS: Knit stitch
- Pattern Repeat
- **C2 Over 2 Left (2/2 LC)** — Sl2 to CN, hold in front. K2, K2 from CN.
- **C2 Over 2 Left P (2/2 LPC)** — Sl2 to CN, hold in front. P2, K2 from CN.
- **C2 Over 2 Right P (2/2 RPC)** — Sl2 to CN, hold in back. K2, P2 from CN.

CORRIE SWEATER
by Sue Gleave

FINISHED MEASUREMENTS
37 (43, 49.25, 55.5, 61.5, 67.75)" finished chest measurement; sweater is meant to be worn with 2-4" of positive ease.

YARN
Knit Picks Wool of the Andes Worsted (100% Peruvian Highland Wool; 110 yards/50g): Brass Heather 25638, 13 (16, 19, 21, 24, 27) balls.

NEEDLES
US 6 (4mm) circular needles plus 16" circular needle or DPN's, or size to obtain gauge.

NOTIONS
Yarn Needle
Stitch Markers
2 Cable Needles
Scrap Yarn or Stitch Holder

GAUGE
26 sts and 28 rows = 4" over Cable Pattern in the rnd and worked flat, blocked.

26 sts and 28 rows = 4" in 2x2 Rib in the rnd and worked flat, blocked.

For pattern support, contact
sue@nativeyarns.co.uk

Notes:

This modern take on a traditional sweater balances deep texture and flowing lines, creating interesting and intricate cables while maintaining a simple, uncluttered style. With the combination of rib and cable, it's a real hug of a sweater, perfect for evenings by the fire or for long bracing walks.

The Corrie Sweater is a generous unisex cable garment, worked in the round from the bottom up and then split at the top of the front and back. The ribbed welt flows into the cable pattern that forms the main part of the body. The sweater is finished with a ribbed neck and sleeves, and designed to be worn with some positive ease.

When working the chart in the rnd, read each row from right to left as a RS row. To work the flat chart, read RS rows (odd numbers) from right to left, and WS rows (even numbers) from left to right.

A tutorial for the Mattress St can be found at:
http://tutorials.knitpicks.com/mattress-stitch/

2x2 Rib (worked over multiples of 4 sts)
All Rnds/Rows: *K2, P2; rep from * to end.

Corrie Cable Pattern (in the rnd over a multiple of 40 sts)
Row 1: *P2, (K2, P2) eight times, 2/2/2 RPC; rep from * to end.
Rnd 2 and all even number Rnds through Rnd 40: K all K sts and P all P sts.
Rnd 3: *P2, (K2, P2) seven times, 2/2/2 RPC, P2, K2; rep from * to end.
Rnd 5: *P2, (K2, P2) six times, 2/2/2 RPC, P2, 2/2/2 RPC; rep from * to end.
Rnd 7: *P2, (K2, P2) five times, 2/2/2 RPC, P2, 2/2/2 RPC, P2, K2; rep from * to end.
Rnd 9: *P2, (K2, P2) six times, 2/2/2 RPC, P2, 2/2/2 RPC; rep from * to end.
Rnd 11: *P2, (K2, P2) five times, 2/2/2 RPC, P2, 2/2/2 RPC, P2, K2; rep from * to end.
Rnd 13: *P2, (K2, P2) six times, 2/2/2 RPC, P2, 2/2/2 RPC; rep from * to end.
Rnd 15: *P2, (K2, P2) five times, 2/2/2 RPC, P2, 2/2/2 RPC, P2, K2; rep from * to end.
Rnd 17: *P2, (K2, P2) six times, 2/2/2 RPC, (P2, K2) twice; rep from * to end.
Rnd 19: *P2, (K2, P2) five times, 2/2/2 RPC, (P2, K2) three times; rep from * to end.
Rnd 21: *P2, 2/2/2 LPC, (P2, K2) eight times; rep from * to end.
Rnd 23: *P2, K2, P2, 2/2/2 LPC, (P2, K2) seven times; rep from * to end.
Rnd 25: *P2, 2/2/2 LPC, P2, 2/2/2 LPC, (P2, K2) six times; rep from * to end.
Rnd 27: *P2, K2, P2, 2/2/2 LPC, P2, 2/2/2 LPC, (P2, K2) five times; rep from * to end.
Rnd 29: *P2, 2/2/2 LPC, P2, 2/2/2 LPC, (P2, K2) six times, P2; rep from * to end.
Rnd 31: *P2, K2, P2, 2/2/2 LPC, P2, 2/2/2 LPC, (P2, K2) five times; rep from * to end.

Rnd 33: *P2, 2/2/2 LPC, P2, 2/2/2 LPC, (P2, K2) six times; rep from * to end.
Rnd 35: *P2, K2, P2, 2/2/2 LPC, P2, 2/2/2 LPC, (P2, K2) five times; rep from * to end.
Rnd 37: *P2, (K2, P2) twice, 2/2/2 LPC, (P2, K2) six times; rep from * to end.
Rnd 39: *P2, (K2, P2) three times, 2/2/2 LPC, (P2, K2) five times; rep from * to end.
Rep Rnds 1-40 for pattern.

Corrie Cable Pattern (worked flat over a multiple of 40 sts)
Row 1: *P1, (K2, P2) eight times, 2/2/2 RPC, P1; rep from * to end.
Row 2 and all even number rows through Row 40: K all K sts and P all P sts as they appear.
Row 3: *P1, (K2, P2) seven times, 2/2/2 RPC, P2, K2, P1; rep from * to end.
Row 5: *P1, (K2, P2) six times, 2/2/2 RPC, P2, 2/2/2 RPC, P1; rep from * to end.
Row 7: *P1, (K2, P2) five times, 2/2/2 RPC, P2, 2/2/2 RPC, P2, K2, P1; rep from * to end.
Row 9: *P1, (K2, P2) six times, 2/2/2 RPC, P2, 2/2/2 RPC, P1; rep from * to end.
Row 11: *P1, (K2, P2) five times, 2/2/2 RPC, P2, 2/2/2 RPC, P2, K2, P1; rep from * to end.
Row 13: *P1, (K2, P2) six times, 2/2/2 RPC, P2, 2/2/2 RPC, P1; rep from * to end.
Row 15: *P1, (K2, P2) five times, 2/2/2 RPC, P2, 2/2/2 RPC, P2, K2, P1; rep from * to end.
Row 17: *P1, (K2, P2) six times, 2/2/2 RPC, (P2, K2) twice, P1; rep from * to end.
Row 19: *P1, (K2, P2) five times, 2/2/2 RPC, (P2, K2) three times, P1; rep from * to end.
Row 21: *P1, 2/2/2 LPC, (P2, K2) eight times, P1; rep from * to end.
Row 23: *P1, K2, P2, 2/2/2 LPC, (P2, K2) seven times, P1; rep from * to end.
Row 25: *P1, 2/2/2 LPC, P2, 2/2/2 LPC, (P2, K2) six times, P1; rep from * to end.
Row 27: *P1, K2, P2, 2/2/2 LPC, P2, 2/2/2 LPC, (P2, K2) five times, P1; rep from * to end.
Row 29: *P1, 2/2/2 LPC, P2, 2/2/2 LPC, (P2, K2) six times, P1; rep from * to end.
Row 31: *P1, K2, P2, 2/2/2 LPC, P2, 2/2/2 LPC, (P2, K2) five times, P1; rep from * to end.
Row 33: *P1, 2/2/2 LPC, P2, 2/2/2 LPC, (P2, K2) six times, P1; rep from * to end.
Row 35: *P1, K2, P2, 2/2/2 LPC, P2, 2/2/2 LPC, (P2, K2) five times, P1; rep from * to end.
Row 37: *P1, (K2, P2) twice, 2/2/2 LPC, (P2, K2) six times, P1; rep from * to end.
Row 39: *P1, (K2, P2) three times, 2/2/2 LPC, (P2, K2) five times, P1; rep from * to end.
Rep Rows 1-40 for pattern.

DIRECTIONS

Body
The body is worked in the rnd, from the bottom up.

Lower Body
CO 240 (280, 320, 360, 400, 440) sts. PM to mark beginning of rnd and join, taking care not to twist sts. Work in 2x2 Rib for 38 (46, 48, 50, 54, 56) rnds, then work in Corrie Cable Pattern for 92 (88, 84, 82, 76, 74) rnds.

Divide for Front and Back
Separation Rnd: Remove M, SL1 st from LH needle to RH needle and PM. Using Corrie Cable Pattern and continuing in pattern for flat knitting, across row then place the last 120 (140, 160, 180, 200, 220) sts worked on a stitch holder for the Back. Make a note of the rnd number you have just worked, so you know where to start in the pattern when working on the Back. Begin working flat, on just the Front sts.

Front Top
Next Row: Turn work (WS facing) and work as per Corrie Cable Pattern, K all K sts and P all P sts.

Next Row (RS): Determine which row of Corrie Cable Pattern you start with for flat knitting. For all sizes, this will correspond to the next RS row after the one you worked in the Separation Rnd. Bear in mind that for sizes 43, 55.5 and 67.75", you will only work half of the last rep on each row. Work in pattern for 32 (34, 36, 38, 42, 44) more rows, to end of Row 6 (4, 2, 2, 40, 40) of the Corrie Cable Pattern.

Shape Front Neck
Row 1 (RS): Work in pattern for 40 (49, 58, 67, 76, 85) sts for Left Shoulder, BO 40 (42, 44, 46, 48, 50) sts, work 40 (49, 58, 67, 76, 85) sts in pattern to end for Right Shoulder. Put Left Shoulder sts on st holder and work Right Shoulder.

Right Shoulder
Row 2 and all WS rows through Row 14: Work in pattern as established.
Row 3 (RS): BO 3 (3, 4, 4, 4, 4) sts, work in pattern to end. 37 (46, 54, 63, 72, 81) sts.
Row 5: BO 3 sts, work in pattern to end. 34 (43, 51, 60, 69, 78) sts.
Row 7: BO 2 (2, 2, 3, 3, 3) sts, work in pattern to end. 32 (41, 49, 57, 66, 75) sts.
Row 9: BO 2 sts, work in pattern to end. 30 (39, 47, 55, 64, 73) sts.
Row 11: BO 1 st, work in pattern to end. 29 (38, 46, 54, 63, 72) sts.
Row 13: BO 0 (0, 1, 1, 1, 1) sts, work in pattern to end. 29 (38, 45, 53, 62, 71) sts.

Size 37" Only: BO all sts.

Sizes (43, 49.25, 55.5, 61.5, 67.76)" Only
Next Row (RS): BO - (0, 0, 0, 1, 1) sts, work in pattern to end. - (38, 45, 53, 61, 70) sts.
Next Row: Work in pattern for - (1, 3, 3, 5, 5) rows.
Next Row: BO all sts.

Left Shoulder
Re-join the yarn to work the Left Shoulder sts with WS facing.
Row 2 (WS): BO 3 (3, 4, 4, 4, 4) sts, work in pattern to end. 37 (46, 54, 63, 72, 81) sts.
Row 3 and all RS rows through Row 13: Work in pattern as established.
Row 4: BO 3 sts, work in pattern to end. 34 (43, 51, 60, 69, 78) sts.
Row 6: BO 2 (2, 2, 3, 3, 3) sts, work in pattern to end. 32 (41, 49, 57, 66, 75) sts.
Row 8: BO 2 sts, work in pattern to end. 30 (39, 47, 55, 64, 73) sts.
Row 10: BO 1 st, work in pattern to end. 29 (38, 46, 54, 63, 72) sts.
Row 12: BO 0 (0, 1, 1, 1, 1) sts, work in pattern to end. 29 (38, 45, 53, 62, 71) sts.

Size 37" Only: Work 1 WS row. BO all sts.

Sizes (43, 49.25, 55.5, 61.5, 67.76)" Only
Next Row (WS): BO - (0, 0, 0, 1, 1) sts, work in pattern to end. - (38, 45, 53, 61, 70) sts.
Next Row: Work in pattern for - (2, 4, 4, 6, 6) rows.
Next Row: BO all sts.

Back
Re-attach yarn with WS of work facing.
Next Row (WS): Work next WS row as per Corrie Cable Pattern, K all K sts and P all P sts.
Next Row (RS): Determine which Row of Corrie Cable Pattern you start with for flat knitting. For sizes 37, 49.25 and 61.5", continue with the RS row that follows on from the one you worked in the Separation Rnd. For sizes 43, 55.5 and 67.75", add 22 to the row number of the row you worked in the Separation Rnd. E.g. If the Separation Rnd row was number 15; 15 + 22 = 37, so start on Row 37. If the last rnd was number 33; 33 + 22 = 55, there is no Row 55, so subtract 40 from 55 = 15, so start on the next row, Row 15. Work in pattern for 40 (44, 46, 48, 52, 54) more rows, to end of Row 16 (34, 12, 32, 10, 30) of the Corrie Cable Pattern.

Shape Back Neck
Row 1 (RS): Work in pattern for 35 (44, 52, 61, 69, 77) sts for Right Shoulder, BO 50 (52, 56, 58, 62, 66) sts, work 35 (44, 52, 61, 69, 77) sts in pattern to end for Left Shoulder. Put Right Shoulder sts on st holder and work Left Shoulder.

Left Shoulder
Row 2 and all WS rows through Row 8: Work in pattern as established.
Row 3 (RS): BO 3 sts, work in pattern to end. 32 (41, 49, 58, 66, 74) sts.
Row 5: BO 2 sts, work in pattern to end. 30 (39, 47, 56, 64, 72) sts.
Row 7: BO 1 (1, 1, 2, 2, 2) sts, work in pattern to end. 29 (38, 46, 54, 62, 70) sts.

Sizes 37, 43" Only: BO all sts.

Sizes 49.25, 55.5, 61.5, 67.75" Only
Next Row: BO - (-, 1, 1, 1, 1) st, work in pattern to end. - (-, 45, 53, 61, 70) sts.
Next Row: Work in pattern for - (-, 1, 1, 3, 3) rows.
Next Row: BO all sts.

Right Shoulder
Re-join the yarn to work the Right Shoulder sts with WS facing.
Row 2 (WS): BO 3 sts, work in pattern to end. 32 (41, 49, 58, 66, 74) sts.
Row 3 and all RS rows through Row 7: Work in pattern as established.
Row 4: BO 2 sts, work in pattern to end. 30 (39, 47, 56, 64, 72) sts.
Row 6: BO 1 (1, 1, 2, 2, 2) sts, work in pattern to end. 29 (38, 46, 54, 62, 70) sts.

Sizes 37, 43" Only: BO all sts.

Sizes 49.25, 55.5, 61.5, 67.75" Only
Next Row: BO - (-, 1, 1, 1, 1) st, work in pattern to end. - (-, 45, 53, 61, 70) sts.
Next Row: Work in pattern for - (-, 2, 2, 4, 4) rows.
Next Row: BO all sts.

Sleeves
The sleeves are worked flat from the wrists up. Incorporate inc sts into the 2x2 Rib pattern.
CO 50 (54, 58, 62, 62, 66) sts. Work in 2x2 Rib for 28 (28, 26, 20, 20, 20) rows.
Next Row (RS): Work in 2x2 Rib, M1 at each end of the row. 52 (56, 60, 64, 64, 68) sts.
Next Row (WS): Work in 2x2 Rib.

Size 37" Only: Work in 2 x 2 Rib for 90 further rows, at the same time inc by 2 sts on every 10**th** row (M1 at each end of row). 70 sts. Work a further 16 rows in 2x2 Rib, with no incs.
Next Row: BO all sts.

Sizes - (49.25, 55.5, 61.5, 67.75)" Only
Work in 2x2 Rib for – (42, 42, 40, 60, 60) further rows, inc by 2 sts on every – (7, **6**, 5, 5, 5)th row (M1 at each end of row). – (68, 74, 80, 88, 92) sts. Work in 2x2 Rib for – (50, 52, 63, 49, 49) further rows, inc by 2 sts on every – (10, 7, 9, 7, 7)th row, - (78, 88, 94, 102, 106) sts. Work a further – (20, 23, 25, 21, 21) rows in 2x2 Rib, with no incs, or desired length to underarm.
Next Row: BO all sts.

Neckband
PU and K 104 (108, 112, 116, 120, 124) sts around the neck. PM for beginning of rnd. Work 20 rnds in 2x2 Rib. BO all sts.
To finish, fold neck over double and sew to secure at inside edge.

Finishing
Weave in ends, wash and block to diagram. Set in Sleeves and sew in, join shoulder seams, sew sleeves seams, using mattress stitch.

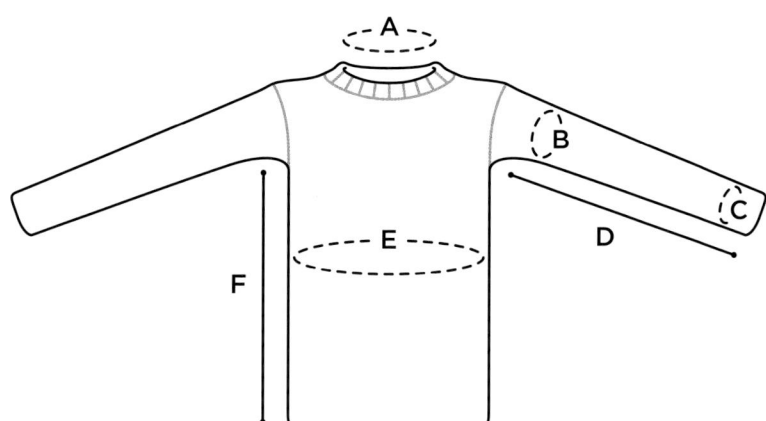

A 16 (16.5, 17.25, 17.75, 18.5, 19)"
B 10.75 (12, 13.5, 14.5, 15.75, 16.5)"
C 7.75 (8.25, 9, 9.5, 9.5, 10.25)"
D 20 (20, 20.5, 21.5, 21.5, 21.5)"
E 37 (43, 49.25, 55.5, 61.5, 67.75)"
F 19 (19, 18.75, 18.5, 18.25, 18.5)"

Corrie Cable Pattern Chart (Round)

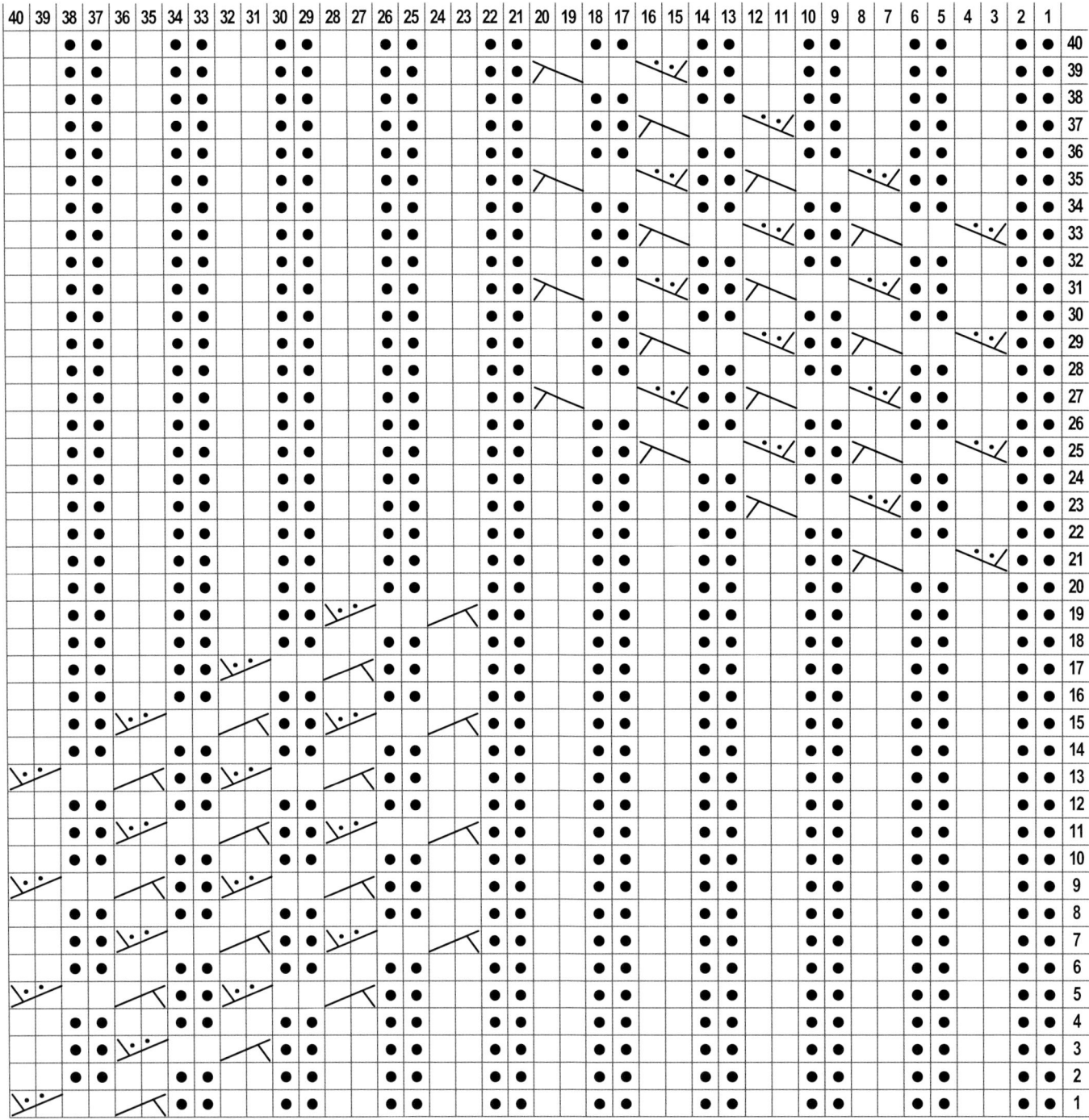

Legend

☐ K
RS: Knit stitch
WS: Purl stitch

● P
RS: Purl stitch
WS: Knit stitch

2/2/2 Left Purl Cross (LPC)
Sl2 to CN, hold in front. Sl next 2 sts to second CN and hold in back. K2, P2 from back CN. K2 from front CN.

2/2/2 Right Purl Cross (RPC)
Sl4 to CN, hold in back. K2, sl2 sts from CN to LH needle and move CN to front. P2, then K2 from CN.

Corrie Cable Pattern Chart (Flat)

GAME THEORY

by Holli Yeoh

FINISHED MEASUREMENTS
41.25 (45.25, 48.25, 51.75, 55.75, 59.25, 63.75, 67.25, 71.75, 75.25)" finished bust measurement; garment is meant to be worn with 11-13" of ease.

YARN
Knit Picks Paragon Sport
(50% Fine Merino, 25% Baby Alpaca, 25% Mulberry Silk; 123 yards/50g): Sagebrush 26968, 12 (14, 14, 15, 17, 18, 19, 20, 21, 22) balls.

NEEDLES
US 6 (4mm) straight or circular needles, or size to obtain gauge.

US 5 (3.75mm) straight or circular needles, or size to obtain gauge.

US 3 (3.25mm) 16" circular or DPN needles, or 3 sizes smaller than needle to obtain gauge on Checked Cable Pattern.

NOTIONS
Yarn Needle
Locking Stitch Markers
Cable Needle
Scrap Yarn or Stitch Holders

GAUGE
26 sts and 33.5 rows = 4" over Checked Cable Pattern with US 6 (4mm) needles, blocked.

20.5 sts and 33 rows = 4" in St st with US 5 (3.75mm) needles, blocked.

For pattern support, contact info@holliyeoh.com

Notes:

Working this cabled checkerboard fabric in luxurious yarn at a loose gauge is a winning strategy, conveying relaxed elegance in a sweater you'll love to wear. The dropped-shoulder silhouette with a lower-in-back split hem is both flattering and comfortable, the contemporary look completed with narrow sleeves and a wide neckline.

The pullover is worked in pieces from the bottom up, with seams lending structure and an exposed three-needle bind-off providing the final touch at the shoulders.

When neck and shoulder shaping cuts through the cabled sections of the Checked Cable Pattern, you may wish to discontinue the cabled stitches and replace them with reverse St st.

A tutorial on Wrap & Turn (W&T) can be found at:
http://tutorials.knitpicks.com/wptutorials/short-rows-wrap-and-turn-or-wt/

A tutorial on the 3-Needle BO can be found at:
http://tutorials.knitpicks.com/3-needle-bind-off/

If working a chart in the rnd, read each row from right to left as a RS row. When working flat, read RS rows (odd numbers) from right to left, and WS rows (even numbers) from left to right.

Mock Ribbing (worked flat over multiple of 3 sts, plus 4)
Row 1 (RS): Knit.
Row 2 (WS): P3, *K1, P2; rep from * to last st, P1.
Rep Rows 1 and 2 for pattern.

Mock Ribbing (worked in the rnd over multiple of 3 sts)
Rnd 1: Knit.
Rnd 2: *K2, P1; rep from * to end of rnd.
Rep Rnds 1 and 2 for pattern.

Checked Cable Pattern (worked flat over 24 sts)
Row 1 (RS): K12, P1, K10, P1.
Row 2 (WS): K1, P10, K1, P2, K8, P2.
Row 3: 2/2 LPC, P4, 2/2 RPC, P1, K10, P1.
Row 4: K1, P10, K3, P2, K4, P2, K2.
Row 5: P2, 2/2 LPC, 2/2 RPC, P3, K10, P1.
Row 6: K1, P10, K5, P4, K4.
Row 7: P4, 2/2 LC, P5, K10, P1.
Row 8: Rep Row 6.
Row 9: P2, 2/2 RPC, 2/2 LPC, P3, K10, P1.
Row 10: Rep Row 4.
Row 11: 2/2 RPC, P4, 2/2 LPC, P1, K10, P1.
Row 12: Rep Row 2.
Rows 13-14: Knit.
Row 15: P1, K10, P1, K12.
Row 16: P2, K8, P2, K1, P10, K1.
Row 17: P1, K10, P1, 2/2 LPC, P4, 2/2 RPC.
Row 18: K2, P2, K4, P2, K3, P10, K1.
Row 19: P1, K10, P3, 2/2 LPC, 2/2 RPC, P2.
Row 20: K4, P4, K5, P10, K1.
Row 21: P1, K10, P5, 2/2 LC, P4.
Row 22: Rep Row 20.
Row 23: P1, K10, P3, 2/2 RPC, 2/2 LPC, P2.
Row 24: Rep Row 18.
Row 25: P1, K10, P1, 2/2 RPC, P4, 2/2 LPC.
Row 26: Rep Row 16.
Rows 27-28: Knit.
Rep Rows 1-28 for pattern.

Bias Bind-Off
The Bias Bind-Off provides a smooth, finished effect for diagonal bind-offs, such as on the neckline, but a traditional bind-off will also work. All slip sts are done as if to purl. After the initial neckline bind off, SL the last st in the row before the next bind off. At beginning of bind off row, SL 2 sts, pass first st over 2nd st, BO remaining sts (if any) in the usual manner.

2/1 LPC: Sl 2 to CN, hold in front, P1, K2 from CN.
2/1 RPC: Sl 1 to CN, hold in back, K2, P1 from CN.
2/2 LC: Sl 2 to CN, hold in front, K2, K2 from CN.
2/2 LPC: Sl 2 to CN, hold in front, P2, K2 from CN.
2/2 RCP: Sl 2 to CN, hold in back, K2, P2 from CN.

Right-Slanting Raised Increase (RRI): With right needle, K into right shoulder of st in row directly below the next st on left needle. 1 st inc.
Left-Slanting Raised Increase (LRI): Use left needle to pick up st 2 rows directly below last st worked and K into it. 1 st inc.

DIRECTIONS

Back
Ribbing
With US 3 (3.25mm) needles, CO 130 (139, 148, 160, 169, 181, 196, 208, 220, 232) sts.
Work Mock Ribbing until piece measures 5.5", ending with a WS row.

Change to US 6 (4mm) needles.
Setup Row 1 (RS): K13 (10, 10, 16, 10, 16, 16, 22, 13, 19), *RRI, K21 (15, 18, 18, 15, 15, 15, 15, 15, 15); rep from * 4 (7, 6, 6, 9, 9, 10, 10, 12, 12) times more, RRI, K12 (9, 12, 18, 9, 15, 15, 21, 12, 18). 136 (148, 156, 168, 180, 192, 208, 220, 234, 246) sts.
Setup Row 2 (WS): P2 (2, 6, 6, 6, 6, 2, 2, 3, 3) sts, K to last 2 (2, 6, 6, 6, 6, 2, 2, 3, 3) sts, P to end.

Begin Checked Cable Pattern
Note: Depending on the size worked, RS rows will end with either a full or half repeat and WS rows will begin with either a full or half repeat, respectively.
Row 1 (RS): K2 (2, 6, 6, 6, 6, 2, 2, 3, 3) sts, work Row 1 of Checked Cable Pattern to last 2 (2, 6, 6, 6, 6, 2, 2, 3, 3) sts, ending with either Stitch 12 or 24, K to end.

Row 2 (WS): P2 (2, 6, 6, 6, 6, 2, 2, 3, 3) sts, work Row 2 of Checked Cable Pattern to last 2 (2, 6, 6, 6, 6, 2, 2, 3, 3) sts, P to end.

Work in pattern as established, completing 5 (4, 5, 4, 4, 4, 4, 4, 4, 4) reps of Checked Cable Pattern Rows 1-28 from ribbing, plus 0 (26, 0, 22, 24, 18, 16, 16, 18, 16) rows more.

Shoulder Shaping

The shoulders are shaped with short rows and worked in pattern throughout. When it's no longer possible to work the cabled section of the rep, work in rev St st.

Short Rows 1 (RS) & 2 (WS): Work to last 8 (7, 8, 7, 6, 6, 6, 6, 7, 7) sts, W&T.

Short Rows 3 & 4: Work to 8 (7, 7, 7, 6, 5, 6, 6, 7, 7) sts before last turn, W&T.

Rep Short Rows 3 & 4 an additional 2 (2, 4, 0, 7, 10, 2, 8, 1, 1) time(s) more.

Sizes 45.25, 51.75, 63.75, 67.25, 71.75, 75.25" ONLY

Short Rows 5 & 6: Work to – (6, –, 6, –, –, 5, 5, 6, 6) sts before last turn, W&T.

Rep Short Rows 5 & 6 an additional – (1, –, 5, –, –, 8, 2, 9, 10) time(s) more.

All Sizes

Next Row (RS): Work to end of row, picking up wraps and working together with wrapped sts.

Next Row (WS): Work 40 (46, 50, 56, 60, 66, 74, 80, 87, 93) sts, BO 56 (56, 56, 56, 60, 60, 60, 60, 60, 60) sts, work remaining 39 (45, 49, 55, 59, 65, 73, 79, 86, 92) sts. 40 (46, 50, 56, 60, 66, 74, 80, 87, 93) sts each shoulder.

Place sts on holder.

Front

With US 3 (3.25mm) needles, CO 130 (139, 148, 160, 169, 181, 196, 208, 220, 232) sts.

Work Mock Ribbing until piece measures 2.5", ending with a WS row.

Work as for Back from Begin Checked Cable Pattern until 4.5 reps have been completed, ending with Row 14 of Checked Cable Pattern.

Left Neck and Shoulder Shaping

Note: For the neck shaping, I recommend using the Bias Bind Off method (see Notes), which provides a smooth edge for curved bind-offs. This method is optional and the traditional bind-off will work as well.

Next Row (RS): Work in pattern for 53 (59, 63, 69, 74, 80, 88, 94, 101, 107) sts, S1 1; turn. Continue on this set of sts only for left neckline and shoulder shaping; place remaining sts on stitch holder or scrap yarn if desired.

Read ahead before you continue. Some neck shaping and shoulder shaping short rows are worked concurrently.

Count rows, beginning with next row, while working neck shaping; begin shoulder shaping after 14 (12, 12, 8, 8, 4, 2, 4, 2, 2) rows are completed.

At beginning of alternate WS rows, BO 3 sts 2 (2, 2, 2, 3, 3, 3, 3, 3, 3) times, then BO 2 sts twice, then BO 1 st 4 (4, 4, 4, 2, 2, 2, 2, 2, 2) times for neck shaping. 40 (46, 50, 56, 60, 66, 74, 80, 87, 93) sts when neck shaping is complete.

After 14 (12, 12, 8, 8, 4, 2, 4, 2, 2) rows of neck shaping, begin shoulder shaping short rows as follows:

Short Rows 1 (WS) & 2 (RS): Work to last 8 (7, 8, 7, 6, 6, 6, 6, 7, 7) sts, W&T. Work to end.

Short Rows 3 & 4: Work to 8 (7, 7, 7, 6, 5, 6, 6, 7, 7) sts before last turn, W&T. Work to end.

Rep Short Rows 3 & 4 an additional 2 (2, 4, 0, 7, 10, 2, 8, 1, 1) time(s) more.

Sizes 45.25, 51.75, 63.75, 67.25, 71.75, 75.25" ONLY

Short Rows 5 & 6: Work to – (6, –, 6, –, –, 5, 5, 6, 6) sts before last turn, W&T. Work to end.

Rep Short Rows 5 & 6 an additional – (1, –, 5, –, –, 8, 2, 9, 10) time(s) more.

All Sizes

40 (46, 50, 56, 60, 66, 74, 80, 87, 93) sts.

Next Row (WS): Work to end of row, picking up wraps and working together with wrapped sts.

Place sts on holder.

Right Neck and Shoulder Shaping

With RS facing, rejoin yarn, BO center 28 (28, 28, 28, 30, 30, 30, 30, 30, 30) sts, work remaining sts in pattern. 54 (60, 64, 70, 75, 81, 89, 95, 102, 108) sts.

Read ahead before you continue. Some neck shaping and shoulder shaping short rows are worked concurrently. Count rows, beginning with next row, while working neck shaping; begin shoulder shaping after 15 (13, 13, 9, 9, 5, 3, 5, 3, 3) rows are completed.

At beginning of alternate RS rows, BO 3 sts 2 (2, 2, 2, 3, 3, 3, 3, 3, 3) times, then BO 2 sts twice, then BO 1 st 4 (4, 4, 4, 2, 2, 2, 2, 2, 2) times for neck shaping. 40 (46, 50, 56, 60, 66, 74, 80, 87, 93) sts when neck shaping is complete.

After 15 (13, 13, 9, 9, 5, 3, 5, 3, 3) rows of neck shaping, begin shoulder shaping short rows as follows:

Short Rows 1 (RS) & 2 (WS): Work to last 8 (7, 8, 7, 6, 6, 6, 6, 7, 7) sts, W&T. Work to end.

Short Rows 3 & 4: Work to 8 (7, 7, 7, 6, 5, 6, 6, 7, 7) sts before last turn, W&T. Work to end.

Rep Short Rows 3 & 4 an additional 2 (2, 4, 0, 7, 10, 2, 8, 1, 1) time(s) more.

Sizes 45.25, 51.75, 63.75, 67.25, 71.75, 75.25" ONLY

Short Rows 5 & 6: Work to – (6, –, 6, –, –, 5, 5, 6, 6) sts before last turn, W&T. Work to end.

Rep Short Rows 5 & 6 and additional – (1, –, 5, –, –, 8, 2, 9, 10) time(s) more.

All Sizes

40 (46, 50, 56, 60, 66, 74, 80, 87, 93) sts.

Next Row (RS): Work to end of row, picking up wraps and working together with wrapped sts.

Place sts on holder.

Sleeve (make two)

With US 3 (3.25mm) needles, CO 43 (43, 43, 43, 46, 46, 46, 46, 46, 46) sts.

Work 6 rows of Mock Ribbing.

Change to US 5 (3.75mm) needles.

Beginning with knit row, work in St st until piece measures 2" from CO, ending with a WS row.

Sleeve Shaping

Inc Row (RS): K2, RRI, K to last 2 sts, LRI, K2. 2 sts inc.

Rep Inc Row every 14 (12, 10, 10, 8, 8, 6, 6, 4, 4) rows 1 (7, 3, 8, 3, 8, 3, 13, 8, 12) time(s) more, then every 16 (14, 12, 12, 10, 10, 8, 8, 6, 6) rows 7 (3, 8, 4, 10, 5, 11, 3, 10, 6) time(s). 61 (65, 67, 69, 74, 74, 76, 80, 84, 84) sts.

Work even in St st until piece measures 19.25 (19.25, 19.25, 19.5, 19, 18, 17, 16.5, 15.25, 14.25)", ending with a WS row.

BO all sts.

Finishing

Wash and gently block pieces to schematic measurements. Holding WS together, join left shoulder seam using 3 Needle Bind-off, working from armhole edge towards neck edge. Join right shoulder seam working P-wise from armhole edge to neck edge.

Place markers 5.75 (6, 6.25, 6.5, 7, 7, 7.25, 7.5, 8, 8)" down from each side of shoulder seams on selvedge edges of Front and Back.

Sew sleeves between markers, matching the center of the sleeve top with the shoulder seam. Using Mattress stitch, sew sleeve seams. Sew side seams from top of ribbing to armhole.

Neck Edging

With RS facing and 16" US 3 (3.25mm) circular needle, PU and K18 (20, 21, 21, 25, 25, 25, 26, 26, 26) along left front neck from shoulder to center front BO, PU and K28 (28, 28, 28, 30, 30, 30, 30, 30, 30) along center front BO, PU and K18 (20, 21, 21, 25, 25, 25, 26, 26, 26) along right front neck to shoulder, PU and K56 (56, 56, 56, 60, 60, 60, 60, 60, 60) along back neck. 120 (124, 126, 126, 140, 140, 140, 142, 142, 142) sts.

PM and join for working in the round.

Sizes 45.25, 67.25, 71.75, 75.25" ONLY: K2tog, K1, P1, *K2, P1; rep from * to end of rnd. Knit 1 rnd. – (123, –, –, –, –, –, 141, 141, 141) sts.

Sizes 55.75, 59.25, 63.76" ONLY: K1, KFB, *K2, P1; rep from * to end of rnd. Knit 1 rnd. – (–, –, –, 141, 141, 141, –, –, –) sts.

All Sizes

Work Mock Ribbing until edging measures 1.75" ending with a knit rnd.

BO loosely in pattern.

Weave in ends. Lightly steam Neck Edging and seams.

Legend

- **K** — RS: Knit stitch / WS: Purl stitch
- **P** (●) — RS: Purl stitch / WS: Knit stitch
- Pattern Repeat
- **C2 Over 2 Left (2/2 LC)** — Sl2 to CN, hold in front. K2, K2 from CN.
- **C2 Over 2 Right P (2/2 RPC)** — Sl2 to CN, hold in back. K2, P2 from CN.
- **C2 Over 2 Left P (2/2 LPC)** — Sl2 to CN, hold in front. P2, K2 from CN.

Mock Ribbing Flat

	7	6	5	4	3	2	1
2				●			
							1

Mock Ribbing Round

3	2	1	
●			2
			1

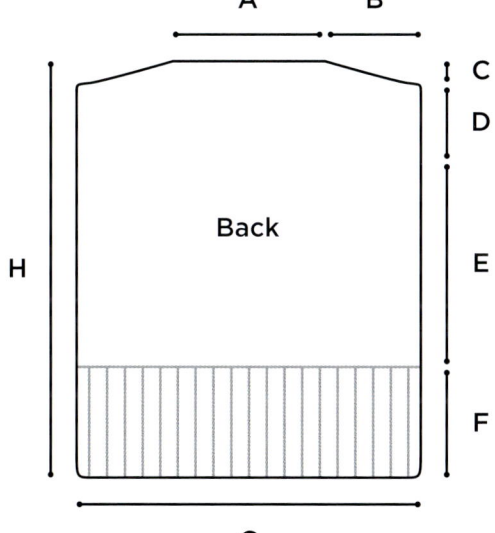

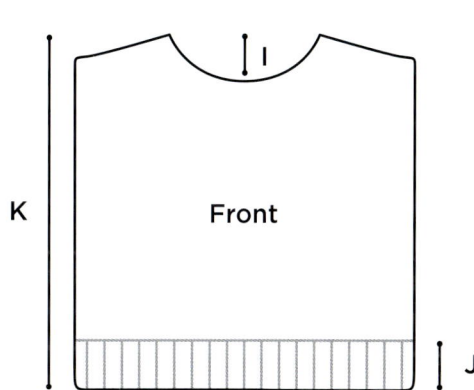

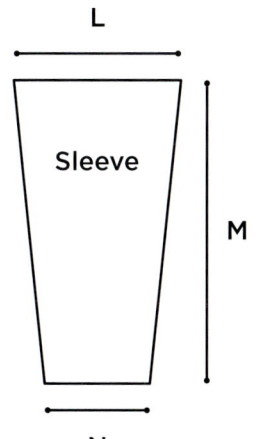

- **A** 8.5 (8.5, 8.5, 8.5, 9.25, 9.25, 9.25, 9.25, 9.25, 9.25)"
- **B** 6.25 (7, 7.75, 8.5, 9.25, 10.25, 11.5, 12.25, 13.5, 14.25)"
- **C** 1.25 (1.75, 1.75, 2.25, 2.5, 3, 3.25, 3.25, 3.25, 3.5)"
- **D** 5.75 (6, 6.25, 6.5, 7, 7, 7.25, 7.5, 8, 8)"
- **E** 11 (10.5, 10.5, 9.75, 9.25, 8.75, 8.25, 8.25, 7.75, 7.5)"
- **F** 5.5"
- **G** 21 (23, 24.5, 26.25, 28.25, 30, 32.25, 34, 36.25, 38)"
- **H** 23.5 (23.75, 24, 24, 24.25, 24.25, 24.25, 24.5, 24.5, 24.5)"
- **I** 2.75 (3, 3.25, 3.25, 3.5, 3.5, 3.5, 3.75, 3.75, 3.75)"
- **J** 2.5"
- **K** 20.5 (20.75, 21, 21, 21.25, 21.25, 21.25, 21.5, 21.5, 21.5)"
- **L** 12 (12.75, 13, 13.5, 14.5, 14.5, 14.75, 15.5, 16.5, 16.5)"
- **M** 19.25 (19.25, 19.25, 19.5, 19, 18, 17, 16.5, 15.25, 14.25)"
- **N** 8.5 (8.5, 8.5, 8.5, 9, 9, 9, 9, 9, 9)"

Checked Cable Pattern Chart

36 Game Theory

HAVANA

by Jill Wright

FINISHED MEASUREMENTS
31.25 (35, 38.5, 43, 47.25, 51, 55.25, 59, 63.25, 67)" finished bust measurement; garment is meant to be worn with approximately 4.5" of ease.

YARN
Knit Picks Gloss DK
(70% Merino Wool, 30% Silk; 123 yards/50g): Cream 24985, 14 (16, 16, 18, 20, 22, 24, 26, 28, 30) balls.

NEEDLES
US 7 (4.5mm) 16" circular needles or DPN's, and straight or 24" or longer circular needles, or size to obtain gauge.

NOTIONS
Yarn Needle
Stitch Markers, including 4 removable
Cable Needle
Scrap Yarn or Stitch Holder

GAUGE
22 sts and 31 rows = 4" in Cable Pattern, blocked.

For pattern support, contact
jill2who@gmail.com

Notes:
Havana is a classic cabled sweater with more than a couple of twists. The longer tunic length is the perfect showcase for this alternating seed stitch and stockinette stitch cable pattern. Add to this the elongated cowl; pull it up over the head as a hood or snood, or fold, roll, or simply push it down around the neck for another cozy look. Fold the lower rib underneath and up to the waist for an ultra-warm classic length look.

The Havana Cable Tunic is a tunic length, drop shoulder sweater with an elongated cowl. The cowl and borders are worked in 2 x 2 rib, the body and sleeves having the all over alternating seed stitch and stockinette cable pattern.

Do not work cable cross unless all 6 sts of cable are present. Cables cross to the right.
The chart is read from right to left on RS rows (odd numbers), and left to right on WS rows (even numbers).

Seed Stockinette Cable Pattern (worked flat over multiple of 16 sts plus 10)
Row 1 (RS): *P2, (K1, P1) 3 times, P2, K6; rep from * to last 10 sts, P2, (K1, P1) 3 times, P2.
Row 2 (WS): *K2, (P1, K1) 3 times, K2, P6; rep from * to last 10 sts, K2, (P1, K1) 3 times, K2.
Row 3: *P2, C3 over 3R; rep from * to last 2 sts, P2.
Row 4: *K2, P6, K2, (P1, K1) 3 times; rep from * to last 10 sts, K2, P6, K2.
Row 5: *P2, K6, P2, (K1, P1); rep from * to last 10 sts, P2, K6, P2.
Rows 6-13: Rep Rows 4-5.
Row 14: Rep Row 4.
Row 15: Rep Row 3.
Row 16: *K2, (P1, K1) 3 times, K2, P6; rep from * to last 10 sts, K2, (P1, K1) 3 times, K2.
Row 17: *P2, (K1, P1) 3 times, P2, K6; rep from * to last 10 sts, P2, (K1, P1) 3 times, P2.
Rows 18-23: Rep Rows 16-17.
Row 24: Rep Row 16.
Rep Rows 1-24 for pattern.

C3 over 3R (3/3 RC): Sl3 to CN, hold in back, K3, K3 from CN.

DIRECTIONS

Back
CO 88 (98, 108, 120, 132, 142, 154, 164, 176, 186) sts.
Rib Row 1 (RS): K1 (2, 1, 1, 2, 2, 1, 1, 2), (P2, K2) across to last 1 (2, 1, 1, 2, 2, 1, 1, 2) st(s), K last st(s).

Rib Row 2 (WS): P1 (2, 1, 1, 1, 2, 2, 1, 1, 2), (K2, P2) across to last 1 (2, 1, 1, 1, 2, 2, 1, 1, 2) st(s), P last st(s).
Rep Rib Rows 1-2 until rib measures 2.5" from CO ending with WS row.

Next Row (RS): P0 (0, 1, 0, 0, 2, 0, 0, 0, 0), work in Seed Stockinette Cable Stitch Pattern from chart beginning with stitch number 2 (5, 1, 2, 4, 1, 1, 4, 6, 1) to last 1 (2, 1, 1, 1, 2, 2, 1, 1, 2) st(s), P to end.
Work in Seed Stockinette Cable Pattern until Back measures 22.5" from CO for all sizes. PM in each end of previous row to mark beginning of armhole.
Work in Seed Stockinette Cable Pattern until back measures 29.5 (29.5, 30, 30, 30.5, 30.5, 31, 31, 31.5, 31.5)" from CO. BO loosely across all sts. Mark center 38 (38, 40, 40, 42, 42, 44, 44, 46, 46) sts for neckline.

Front
Work as for Back until Front measures 27 (27, 27.5, 27.5, 27.5, 27.5, 28, 28, 28, 28)" from CO, ending with WS row.

Shape Left Neck
Dec Row 1 (RS): Work in pattern across 32 (37, 41, 47, 52, 57, 62, 67, 72, 77) sts, PM, K2tog, K1. Turn. 34 (39, 43, 49, 54, 59, 64, 69, 74, 79) sts for Left Neck.
Dec Row 2 (WS): P1, P2tog, SM, pattern across. 33 (38, 42, 48, 53, 58, 63, 68, 73, 78) sts.
Dec Row 3 (RS): Pattern to M, SM, K2tog, K1. 1 st dec.
Dec Row 4 (WS): P1, P2tog, SM, pattern across. 1 st dec.
Rep Dec Rows 3-4 3 more times, until there are 25 (30, 34, 40, 45, 50, 55, 60, 65, 70) sts.
WE until Front measures same as Back at shoulder ending with WS row. BO all sts.

Shape Right Neck
With RS facing, Sl next 18 (18, 20, 20, 22, 22, 24, 24, 26, 26) sts to st holder, join in yarn.
Dec Row 1 (RS): K1, SSK, PM, work across next 32 (37, 41, 47, 52, 57, 62, 67, 72, 77) sts. 1 st dec, 34 (39, 43, 49, 54, 59, 64, 69, 74, 79) sts.
Dec Row 2 (WS): Work across to M, SM, SSP, P1. 1 st dec, 33 (38, 42, 48, 53, 58, 63, 68, 73, 78) sts.
Rep Dec Rows 1-2 4 more times until there are 25 (30, 34, 40, 45, 50, 55, 60, 65, 70) sts.
WE until Front measures same as Back at shoulder ending with WS row. BO all sts.

Sleeves (make 2 the same)
The sleeves are worked flat from the wrists up.
CO 42 (42, 46, 46, 50, 50, 54, 54, 58, 58) sts.
Rib Row 1 (RS): (K2, P2) across to last 2 sts, K2.

Rib Row 2 (WS): (P2, K2) across to last 2 sts, P2.
Rep Rib Rows 1-2 until rib measures 2.5" for all sizes ending with RS row.

Inc Row (WS): KFB next 3 (3, 1, 1, 0, 0, 0, 0, 0) sts, P0 (0, 0, 0, 1, 1, 3, 3, 5, 5), (KFB, K1) across to last 3 (3, 1, 1, 0, 0, 0, 0, 0) sts, KFB remaining sts. 66 (66, 70, 70, 74, 74, 78, 78, 82, 82) sts. Work 14 (14, 14, 14, 14, 14, 2, 2, 2, 2) rows in Seed Stockinette Cable Pattern from chart beginning at st number 5 (5, 3, 3, 1, 1, 15, 15, 5, 5).

*Inc Row (RS): KFB in next st, pattern across to last st, KFB. 2 sts inc.
Work 11 (11, 11, 11, 11, 11, 7, 7, 7, 7) rows in Seed Stockinette Cable Pattern as established.
Rep from * until st count is 78 (78, 84, 84, 90, 90, 96, 96, 100, 100) sts, incorporating new sts into Seed Stockinette Cable Pattern.

Work even until sleeve measures 21.5 (21.25, 20.5, 20, 19.25, 18.5, 17.75, 17, 15.75, 15)", or desired length from CO.

BO all sts loosely.
Block to diagram. Sew shoulder seams.

Neck

Using circular needle or DPNs and beginning at left shoulder seam with RS facing, PU and K 20 (20, 20, 20, 22, 22, 22, 22, 24, 24) sts down left neck, replace 18 (18, 20, 20, 22, 22, 24, 24, 26, 26) sts from st holder across front neck onto needle, PU and K 20 (20, 20, 20, 22, 22, 22, 22, 24, 24) sts up right neck, and 38 (38, 40, 40, 42, 42, 44, 44, 46, 46) sts between markers placed across back neck. 96 (96, 100, 100, 108, 108, 112, 112, 120, 120) sts, PM.
Work in rnds as follows: *K2, P2; rep from * around, SM. Continue working 2 x 2 rib in rnds until neck measures 20" from PU rnd. BO all sts loosely.

Finishing

Sew sleeves between stitch markers on Back and Front. Sew sleeve and side seams. Weave in ends, wash and block to diagram.

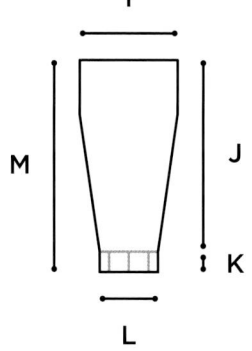

A 4.5 (5.5, 6.25, 7.25, 8.25, 9, 10, 11, 11.75, 12.75)"
B 7 (7, 7.25, 7.25, 7.75, 7.75, 8, 8, 8.25, 8.25)"
C 2.5 (2.5, 2.5, 2.5, 3, 3, 3, 3, 3.5, 3.5)"
D 7 (7, 7.5, 7.5, 8, 8, 8.5, 8.5, 9, 9)"
E 20"
F 2.5"
G 16 (17.75, 19.75, 21.75, 24, 25.75, 28, 29.75, 32, 33.75)"
H 29.5 (29.5, 30, 30, 30.5, 30.5, 31, 31, 31.5, 31.5)"
I 14.25 (14.25, 15.25, 15.25, 16.25, 16.25, 17.5, 17.5, 18.25, 18.25)"
J 19 (18.75, 18, 17.5, 16.75, 16, 15.25, 14.5, 13.25, 12.5)"
K 2.5"
L 7.75 (7.75, 8.25, 8.25, 9, 9, 9.75, 9.75, 10.5, 10.5)"
M 21.5 (21.25, 20.5, 20, 19.25, 18.5, 17.75, 17, 15.75, 15)"

Note: Measurements include seam allowances

Seed Stockinette Cable Pattern Chart

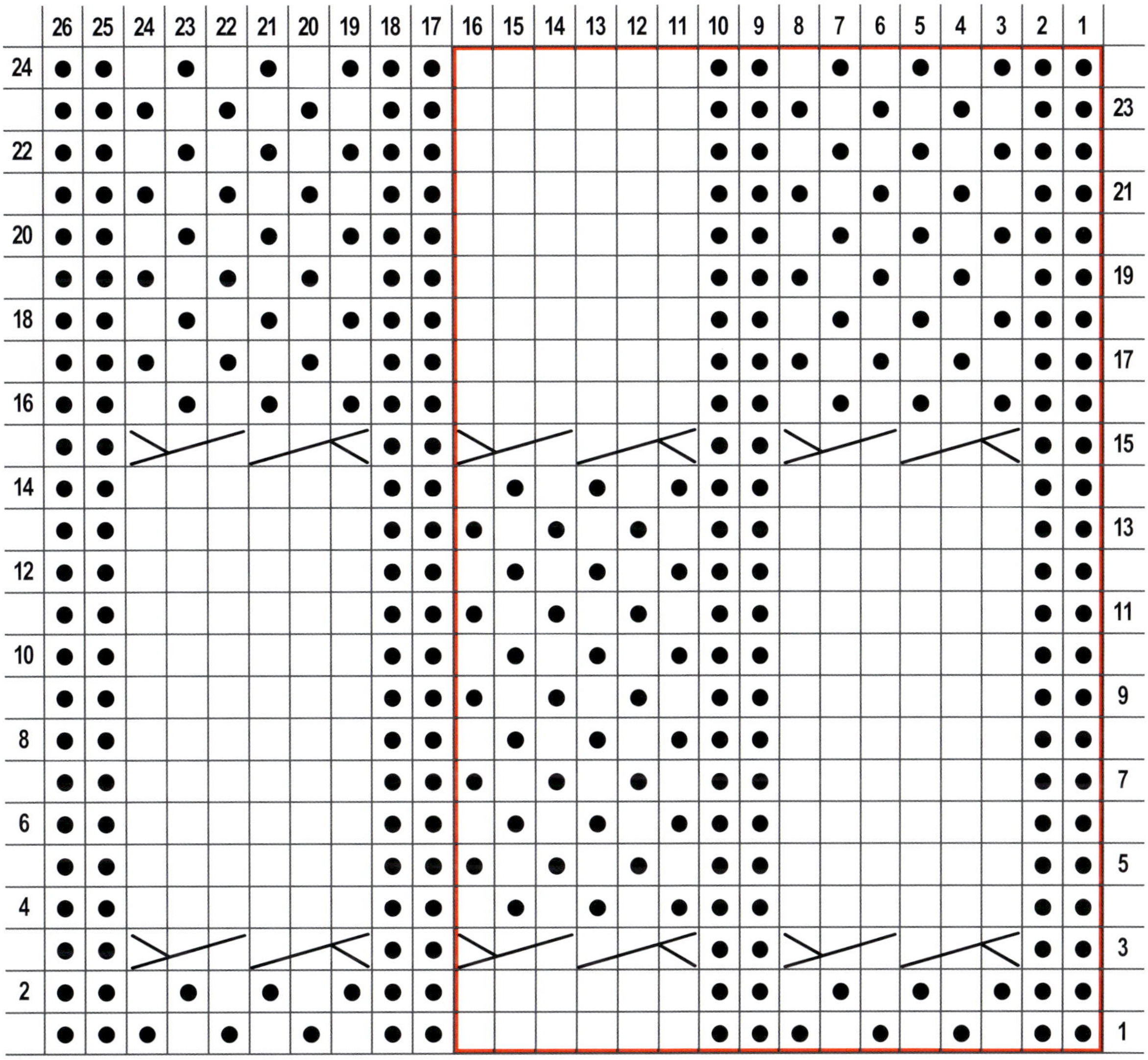

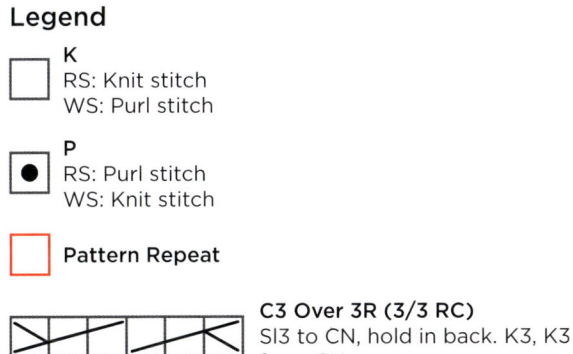

Legend

K
RS: Knit stitch
WS: Purl stitch

P
RS: Purl stitch
WS: Knit stitch

Pattern Repeat

C3 Over 3R (3/3 RC)
Sl3 to CN, hold in back. K3, K3 from CN.

PASSAGE CARDIGAN

by Stacey Gerbman

FINISHED MEASUREMENTS
36.25 (40.5, 44.25, 48.25, 52, 56)" finished bust measurement, buttoned; garment is meant to be worn with 2-4" of positive ease.

YARN
Knit Picks Simply Wool Worsted (100% Eco Wool; 218 yards/100g): Winkle 27473, 5 (6, 7, 8, 9, 10) balls.

NEEDLES
US 8 (5mm) 16, 32, and 40" circular needles, or size to obtain gauge.

US 6 (4mm) 16, 32, and 40" circular needles, or size to obtain gauge.

NOTIONS
Yarn Needle
Stitch Markers
Scrap Yarn or Stitch Holder
(6) 1" Buttons

GAUGE
17 sts and 29 rows = 4" in Gull and Garter Stitch on larger needles, blocked.

22 sts and 28 rows = 4" in K1, P1 Rib on smaller needles, blocked.

For pattern support, contact staceygerbman@gmail.com

Notes:
The body of this cardigan is knit flat to the armholes, then the two front sections and the back are worked separately to the shoulder. The sleeves are worked flat, and then seamed and sewn into the body armholes. The front bands and collar are picked up and knit back and forth.

The Passage Cardigan is worked back and forth on circular needles to handle the large number of stitches. There is subtle A line shaping that happens in garter sections that are wider at the hip and narrow from decreases as you get to the armholes. Instructions have you place markers at the beginning and the end of the Gull and Garter stitch pattern sections, as well as a marker at the side seam. It would be best to use different colored markers to designate the side seam. As you bind off stitches for the shoulder and neck, as soon as you begin to decrease into a Gull section of the Gull and Garter pattern, work the rest of the chart section as if it were Stockinette stitch.

Garter Stitch (worked flat over any number of sts)
All Rows: Knit.

K1, P1 Rib (worked flat over multiple of 2 sts)
Row 1 (RS): *K1, P1, rep from * to the end of row.
Row 2 (WS): *P1, K1, rep from * to the end of row.
Rep Rows 1-2 for pattern.

Knit 1 under loose strand (K1 uls): Insert right needle under loose strand and then into the next st K-wise, from front to back. Knit st normally then bring new st out from under the strand.

Gull and Garter Stitch (worked flat over multiples of 8 sts for body and sleeves)
Row 1 (WS): *K3, P5; rep from * across.
Row 2 (RS): *Sl 5 WYIF, K3; rep from * across.
Row 3: *K3, P5; rep from * across.
Row 4: *K2, K1 uls, K5; rep from * across.
Rep Rows 1-4 for pattern.

Sloped Bind Off
Step 1: Work the first BO rows at the garment edges as usual.
Step 2: One row before the next BO row, work to the last st of the row, turn.
Step 3: Sl the first st from the LH needle P-wise, pass the unworked st of the previous row over the slipped st (the first st is bound off). BO remaining sts as usual.
Rep Steps 2-3 for remaining BO rows.

Backward Loop CO: *Use the working yarn to make a loop around your left thumb, then place this loop onto the RH needle; rep from * until you have the required number of sts on your needle.

DIRECTIONS

Body
CO 209 (229, 251, 273, 295, 317) sts with smaller 32" or 40" circular needle.
Row 1 (WS): P1, *K1, P1; rep from * across.
Row 2 (RS): K1, *P1, K1; rep from * across.

Rep Rows 1-2 until piece measures 4" from CO edge ending with a RS row.
Switch to larger 32" or 40" needle.
Dec Row (WS): P all sts, dec 48 (50, 54, 56, 66, 72) sts evenly across row. 161 (179, 197, 217, 229, 245) sts.

Torso

Set-up Row (RS): K3, PM(1), work Row 2 of Gull and Garter Stitch across next 32 (32, 32, 40, 48, 48) sts, PM(2), K4 (8, 12, 8, 4, 8), PM(3), K7 (12, 15, 11, 8, 7), PM(4), work Row 2 of Gull and Garter Stitch across next 72 (72, 80, 96, 104, 112) sts, PM(5), K4 (9, 8, 8, 7, 8), PM(6), K7 (11, 15, 11, 7, 11), PM(7), Work Row 2 of Gull and Garter Stitch across next 32 (32, 32, 40, 48, 48) sts.

Work across sts, following pattern as set. Maintain the sts before first M in Garter st. Maintain sts between M's 2-4 and 5-7 in Garter st. M 3 and M 6 represent side seams. Cont working in pattern for the next 21 rows ending on a WS row.

Dec Row (RS): K3, SM(1), work in established Gull and Garter Stitch across 32 (32, 32, 40, 48, 48) sts, SM(2), K2 (6, 10, 6, 2, 6), SSK, SM(3), K2tog, K5 (10, 13, 9, 6, 5), SM(4), work in established Gull and Garter Stitch across 72 (72, 80, 96, 104, 112) sts, SM(5), K2 (7, 6, 6, 5, 6), SSK, SM(6), K2tog, K5 (9, 13, 9, 5, 9), SM(7), work in established Gull and Garter Stitch across 32 (32, 32, 40, 48, 48) sts. 4 sts dec.

Work Dec Row every 22nd row 3 (3, 3, 4, 3, 3) more times, decreasing before and after M's 3 and 6. 145 (163, 181, 197, 213, 229) sts.

Work in pattern until piece measures 19" from CO edge or desired length to underarm, ending with a WS row.

Divide for Fronts and Back

Work as established across first 35 (39, 43, 47, 51, 55) sts for right front, transfer next 75 (85, 95, 103, 111, 119) sts to stitch holder or scrap yarn for back, then transfer last 35 (39, 43, 47, 51, 55) sts to separate stitch holder or scrap yarn for left front.

Right Front
Shape Armhole and Front Neck

Armhole and neck shaping occur at the same time. Armhole shaping will begin first on next WS row, and will continue during neck shaping. Please read the following section through to the end, and review Sloped Bind Off before proceeding.

Armhole Shaping: BO 3 (4, 4, 4, 4, 4) sts at the beginning of the next and following WS row, then BO 3 (3, 4, 4, 4, 4) sts at the beginning of the following WS row, then BO 0 (2, 3, 3, 3, 4) sts at the beginning of the following WS row, then BO 0 (0, 2, 2, 3, 3) st at the beginning of the following WS row, then BO 0 (0, 0, 0, 3, 3) sts at the beginning of the following WS row.

At the same time, after first WS row, shape neck as follows:
Neck Dec Row (RS): K1, SSK, work as established to end, 1 st dec at neck edge.
Rep the Neck Dec Row every 6th RS row 0 (0, 3, 0, 1, 0) more times, then every 4th row 10 (11, 7, 12, 11, 13) times, then every RS row 1 (0, 0, 0, 0, 0) times, keeping 1 st at neck edge in Garter St.

Upon completion of all shaping, you will have bound off a total of 9 (13, 17, 17, 21, 22) sts at armhole edge and will have worked the Neck Dec Row a total of 12 (12, 11, 13, 13, 14) times. 14 (14, 15, 17, 17, 19) sts remain for shoulder.

Work even as established over remaining sts until armhole measures 8 (8.5, 9, 9, 9.5, 9.5)" ending with a RS row.

Shape Shoulder
Use the sloped Bind Off in this section for best results.
BO 3 (3, 3, 4, 4, 4) sts at the beginning of the next 3 WS rows, then BO 3 (3, 3, 3, 3, 4) sts at the beginning of following WS row, then BO remaining 2 (2, 3, 2, 2, 3) sts at the beginning of the following WS row.

Back
Transfer held 75 (85, 95, 103, 111, 119) back sts to needle and rejoin yarn ready to work a RS row.

Shape Armholes
Use the Sloped Bind Off in this section for best results.
BO 3 (4, 4, 4, 5, 5) sts at the beginning of the next 4 rows, then BO 3 (3, 4, 4, 4, 5) sts at the beginning of the following 2 rows, then BO 0 (2, 4, 4, 4, 4) sts at the beginning of the following 2 rows, then BO 0 (0, 2, 2, 3, 3) st at the beginning of the following WS row, then BO 0 (0, 0, 0, 3, 3) sts at the beginning of the next WS row. 57 (59, 61, 69, 69, 75) sts.
Work even as established over remaining sts until armhole measures 8 (8.5, 9, 9, 9.5, 9.5)" ending with a WS row.

Shape Shoulders
Use the Sloped Bind Off in this section for best results.
BO 3 (3, 3, 4, 4, 4) sts at the beginning of the next 6 rows, then then BO 3 (3, 3, 3, 3, 4) sts at the beginning of the following 2 rows, then BO 2 (2, 3, 2, 2, 3) sts at the beginning of the following 2 rows.
Transfer remaining 29 (31, 31, 35, 35, 37) sts to stitch holder or scrap yarn for back neck.

Left Front
Transfer held 35 (39, 43, 47, 51, 55) left front sts to needle and rejoin yarn ready to work a RS row.

Shape Armhole and Front Neck
Armhole and neck shaping are worked at the same time. Armhole shaping will begin first on the next row, and will continue during neck shaping. Please read the following section through to the end. Please review Sloped Bind Off before proceeding.

BO 3 (4, 4, 4, 4, 4) sts at the beginning of the next and following RS row, then BO 3 (3, 4, 4, 4, 4) sts at the beginning of the following RS row, then BO 0 (2, 3, 3, 3, 3) sts at the beginning of the following RS row, then BO 0 (0, 2, 2, 3, 3) st at the beginning of the following RS row, then BO 0 (0, 0, 0, 3, 3) sts at the beginning of the following RS row.

At the same time, after the first RS row, shape neck as follows:
Neck Decrease Row (WS): K1, SSP, work as established to end. 1 st dec at neck edge.
Rep the Neck Decrease Row every 6th WS row 0 (0, 3, 0, 1, 0) more times, then every 4th row 10 (11, 7, 12, 11, 13) times, then every WS row 1 (0, 0, 0, 0, 0) times, keeping 1 st at neck edge in Garter St.

Upon completion of all shaping, you will have bound off a total of 9 (13, 17, 17, 21, 22) sts at armhole edge and will have worked the Neck Decrease Row a total of 12 (12, 11, 13, 13, 14) times. 14 (14, 15, 17, 17, 19) sts remain for shoulder.
Work even as established over remaining sts until armhole measures 8 (8.5, 9, 9, 9.5, 9.5)" ending with a RS row.

Shape Shoulder
Use the sloped Bind Off in this section for best results.
BO 3 (3, 3, 4, 4, 4) sts at the beginning of the next 3 RS rows, then BO 3 (3, 3, 3, 3, 4) sts at the beginning of following RS row, then BO remaining 2 (2, 3, 2, 2, 3) sts at the beginning of the following RS row.

Sleeves (make 2)
Loosely, with smaller 16" circular needle, CO 48 (48, 52, 52, 56, 60) sts.
Work K1, P1 Rib for 2", ending with a RS row.
Switch to larger needles.
Dec Row (WS): P all sts decreasing 11 (11, 12, 12, 12, 14) sts evenly across row. 37 (37, 40, 40, 44, 46) sts.
Set Up Row: K3 (3, 5, 5, 3, 4), PM(1), work row 2 of Gull and Garter Stitch across next 32 (32, 32, 32, 40, 40) sts, PM(2), K2 (2, 3, 3, 1, 2) sts.

Shape Sleeve
Sleeve Inc Row (RS): K1, M1R, work as established to last st, M1L, K1. 2 sts inc.
Work a Sleeve Inc Row every 12th row 1 (0, 0, 0, 0, 0) 1 more time, then every 10th row 7 (5, 3, 0, 3, 0) times, then every 8th row 0 (4, 7, 11, 7, 11) times.
Upon completion of this section you will have worked the Sleeve Inc Row a total of 9 (10, 11, 12, 11, 12) times. 55 (57, 62, 64, 66, 70) sts.
Work even in established pattern until piece measures 18 (18, 18.5, 18.5, 18.5, 18.75)" or desired length to underarm from CO edge, ending with a WS row.

Shape Cap
Use the Sloped Bind Off in this section for best results.
BO 3 (4, 4, 4, 4, 4) sts at the beginning of the next 4 rows, then BO 3 (3, 4, 4, 4, 4) sts at the beginning of the following 2 rows, then BO 0 (2, 3, 3, 3, 4) sts at the beginning of the following 2 rows. 37 (31, 32, 34, 36, 38) sts.
Knit in pattern for 0.5 (0.75, 1, 1.25, 1.25, 1.25)"

Cap Dec Row (RS): K1, K2tog, work as established to last 3 sts, SSK, K1. 2 sts dec.
Rep the Cap Dec Row every 4th row 0 (0, 1, 1, 2, 3) more times, then every RS row
12 (9, 8, 9, 8, 7) times. 11 (11, 12, 12, 14, 16) sts.
BO all sts in pattern.

Finishing

Weave in ends, wash and block to diagram. Sew shoulder seams. Sew sleeve seams. Set in sleeves.

Collar

With smaller 40" circular needle, RS facing and beginning at bottom of right front edge, PU and K 104 sts evenly up right front to first neck decrease, PU and K 44 (46, 49, 49, 51, 51) sts up right front neck edge to shoulder; transfer 29 (31, 31, 35, 35, 37) held back needle sts to LH needle tip and K across; PU and K 44 (46, 49, 49, 51, 51) sts down left front neck edge ending at first neck decrease, PM (2), PU and K 104 sts down left front edge ending at CO edge. 325 (331, 337, 341, 345, 347) sts.

Row 1: P1, *K1, P1; rep from * to end.
Row 2: K1, *P1, K1; rep from * to end.

Rep Rows 1-2 2 more times.
Rep Row 1 once more.
Buttonhole Row 1: K1, P1 Rib for 18 sts, *BO 2 sts, K1, P1 Rib for 12 sts; rep from * 5 more times, BO 2, cont in K1, P1 Rib to end.
Buttonhole Row 2: Cont in established rib, CO 2 sts using the Backwards Loop CO method over BO sts from Buttonhole Row 1.
Work back and forth in K1, P1 Rib until band measures 2" ending with a WS row.
Next Row (RS): BO all sts.

Weave in any remaining ends invisibly on the WS of fabric. Gently steam collar or wet-block entire garment again. Sew on buttons opposite buttonholes.

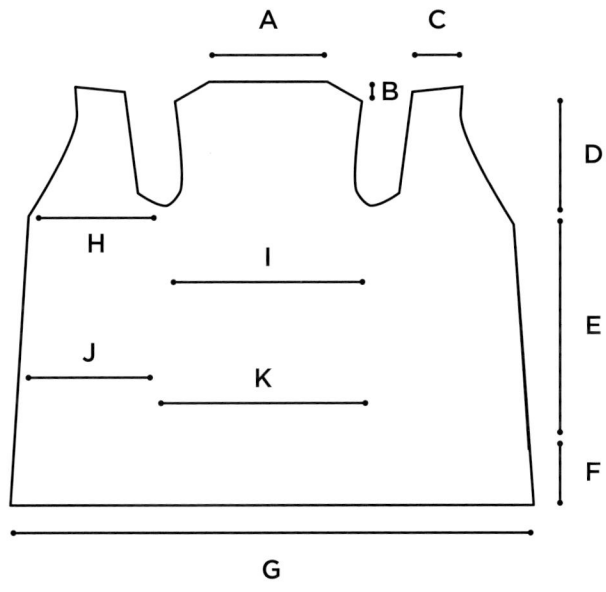

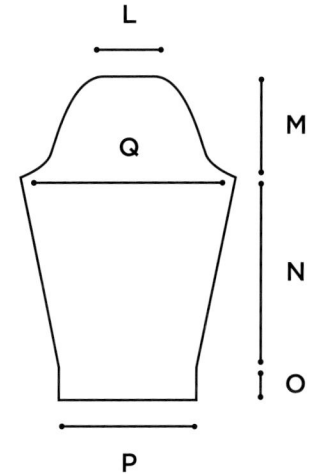

- A (Back Neck Width) 6.75 (7.25, 7.25, 8.25, 8.25, 8.75)"
- B (Front Neck Drop) 1.5"
- C (Shoulder Width) 3.25 (3.25, 3.5, 4, 4, 4.5)"
- D (Armhole Length) 8 (8.5, 9, 9, 9.5, 9.5)"
- E (Body Length) 15"
- F (Ribbing Length) 4"
- G (Hip Measurement, No Bands) 38 (41.75, 45.75, 49.75, 53.75, 57.75)"
- H (Upper Front Measurement) 8.25 (9.25, 10, 11, 12, 13)"
- I (Upper Back Measurement) 17.75 (20, 22.25, 24.25, 26, 28)"
- J (Lower Front Measurement) 9.25 (10, 11, 12, 13, 14)"
- K (Lower Back Measurement) 19.5 (22, 24.25, 27, 28, 30)
- L (Sleeve Cap Width) 2.5 (2.5, 2.75, 2.75, 3.25, 3.75)"
- M (Sleeve Cap Height) 5.25 (5, 5.5, 6, 6.25, 6.5)"
- N (Sleeve Length) 16 (16, 16.5, 16.5, 16.5, 16.75)"
- O (Ribbing Length) 2"
- P (Sleeve Cuff) 8.75 (8.75, 9.5, 9.5, 10.25, 11)"
- Q (Upper Arm) 13 (13.5, 14.5, 15, 15.5, 16.5)"

Note: Measurements do not include 2" buttonbands.

PLAIT PULLOVER
by Stacey Gerbman

FINISHED MEASUREMENTS
36 (39, 42, 45, 48, 51)" finished bust measurement; garment is meant to be worn with 2-4" of positive ease.

YARN
Knit Picks Stroll Sock
(75% Fine Superwash Merino Wool, 25% Nylon; 231 yards/50g): Dove Heather 25023, 4 (5, 5, 6, 6, 7) balls.

Knit Picks Alpaca Cloud Fingering
(100% Superfine Alpaca, 200yards/50g): Sophia 26912, 6 (7, 7, 8, 8, 9) hanks.

NEEDLES
US 8 (5mm) 16, 32, and 40" circular needles, or size to obtain gauge.

US 6 (4mm) 16, 32, and 40" circular needles, or size to obtain gauge.

NOTIONS
Yarn Needle
Cable Needle
Stitch Markers
Scrap Yarn or Stitch Holder

GAUGE
24 sts and 27 rows = 4" in Plait Cable pattern with yarn held double on larger needles, blocked.

28 sts and 28 rows = 4" in K2, P2 Rib with yarn held double on smaller needles, blocked.

16 sts and 34 rows = 4" in Garter st with yarn held double on larger needles, blocked.

For pattern support, contact
staceygerbman@gmail.com

Notes:
The body of this pullover is knit bottom up in the round to the armholes, holding a strand of Stroll Sock and Alpaca Cloud together. The front and back are then worked separately in Garter stitch, holding two strands of Alpaca Cloud together. The sleeves are worked flat, and then seamed and sewn into the body armholes. Stitches are picked up around the neck to finish in K2 P2 Rib.

When working the flat chart, read RS rows (odd numbers) from right to left, and WS rows (even numbers) from left to right. When working the chart in the rnd, read all rows from right to left, as a RS row.

Garter Stitch (worked flat over any number of sts)
All Rows: Knit.

K2, P2 Rib (worked flat over multiples of 4 sts)
Row 1 (RS): *K2, P2, rep from * to the end of row.
Row 2 (WS): *K2, P2, rep from * to the end of row.
Rep Rows 1-2 for pattern.

K2, P2 Rib (worked in the rnd over multiples of 4 sts)
Rnd 1: *K2, P2, rep from * to end of row.
Rep Rnd 1 for pattern.

Plait Cable Pattern (worked flat over multiples of 18 sts)
Row 1 (RS): *K3, c3 over 3 right, c3 over 3 left, K3; rep from * to end.
Row 2 (WS): P across all sts.
Row 3: K across all sts.
Row 4: Rep Row 2.
Rows 5-8: Rep Rows 1-4.
Row 9: *C3 over 3 left, K6, c3 over 3 right; rep from * to end.
Rows 10-12: Rep Rows 2-4.
Rows 13-16: Rep Rows 9-12.
Rep Rows 1-16 for pattern.

Plait Cable Pattern (worked in the rnd over multiples of 18 sts)
Rnd 1: *K3, c3 over 3 right, c3 over 3 left, K3; rep from * to end.
Rnds 2-4: K across all sts.
Rnds 5-8: Rep Rnds 1-4.
Rnd 9: *C3 over 3 left, K6, c3 over 3 right; rep from * to end.
Rnds 10-12: K across all sts.
Rnds 13-16: Rep Rnds 9-12.
Rep Rnds 1-16 for pattern.

Sloped Bind Off
Step 1: Work the first BO rows at the garment edges as usual.
Step 2: One row before the next BO row, work to the last st of the row, turn.
Step 3: Sl the first st from the LH needle P-wise, pass the unworked st of the previous row over the slipped st (the first st is bound off). BO remaining sts as usual.
Rep Steps 2-3 for remaining BO rows.

DIRECTIONS

Body
Using one strand of Stroll Sock and one strand of Alpaca Cloud held together, loosely CO 252 (272, 292, 312, 336, 356) sts with smaller size 32" or 40" circular needle. PM and join in the rnd being careful not to twist sts.
Work in K2, P2 Rib until piece measures 2" from CO edge. Switch to larger size 32" or 40" needle.
Dec Row: K all sts, decreasing 36 (38, 40, 42, 48, 50) sts evenly across rnd. 216 (234, 252, 270, 288, 306) sts.

Torso
Begin following Plait Cable pattern in the rnd from the chart or written directions. Work Plait Cable pattern until piece measures 15" from CO edge, or desired length to underarm.

Divide for Front and Back
Next Row: BO 4 sts, K across 104 (113, 122, 131, 140, 149) sts for the front, transfer next 108 (117, 126, 135, 144, 153) sts to stitch holder or scrap yarn for back.

Front
Shape Raglan and Front Neck
Raglan shaping continues while neck shaping is happening. Please read the following section through to the end, and review Sloped Bind Off before proceeding.
Next Row (WS): BO 4 sts, P across all sts, break Stroll Sock yarn. 100 (109, 118, 127, 136, 145) sts.

Begin working in Garter St, using 2 strands of Alpaca Cloud held together.
Set-up Row 1 (RS): K all sts, decreasing 34 (37, 40, 43, 40, 49) sts evenly across. 66 (72, 78, 84, 96, 96) sts.
Row 2 (WS): K across all sts.

Begin Raglan Shaping
Raglan Shaping Row (RS): K2tog, K across to last 2 sts, SSK. 2 sts dec.
Cont in Garter st and rep Raglan Shaping Row every 4th row 7 (5, 5, 5, 2, 5) more times, then every RS row 17 (21, 23, 25, 33, 29) times.

At the same time, when there are 26 (28, 30, 32, 34, 36) sts, begin to shape neck as follows:
Right Front Neck
Next Row (RS): K2tog, K 11 (12, 13, 14, 15, 16) place the next 13 (14, 15, 16, 17, 18) sts on a holder for Left Front Neck.
Row 1 (WS): BO 3 (3, 4, 4, 4, 4), K to end.
Row 2 (RS): K2tog, K across to last st, turn leaving last st on needle.
Row 3: BO 2 (2, 2, 2, 2, 3) sts, K to end.
Row 4: K2tog, K across to last st, turn leaving last st on needle.
Row 5: BO 1 (2, 2, 2, 2, 3) sts, K to end.
Row 6: K2tog, K across to last st, turn leaving st on the needle.
Row 7: BO 1 (1, 1, 2, 2, 2) sts, K to end.
Row 8: K2tog.
Row 9: BO all sts.

Left Front Neck
Move the 13 (14, 15, 16, 17, 18) sts from holder and place them back onto the needle. Join yarn at the center front neck, ready to begin a RS row.
Row 1 (RS): BO 3 (3, 4, 4, 4, 4), K to end.
Row 2 (WS): SSK, K across to last st, turn leaving last st on needle.
Row 3: BO 2 (2, 2, 2, 2, 3) sts, K to end.
Row 4: SSK, K across to last st, turn leaving last st on needle.
Row 5: BO 1 (2, 2, 2, 2, 3) sts, K to end.
Row 6: SSK, K across to last st, turn leaving st on the needle.
Row 7: BO 1 (1, 1, 2, 2, 2) sts, K to end.
Row 8: SSK, K across to last st, turn leaving last st on needle.
Row 9: BO all sts.

Back
Transfer held 108 (117, 126, 135, 144, 153) back sts to needle and rejoin yarn ready to work a RS row.
Row 1 (RS): BO 4, K across all sts.
Row 2 (WS): BO 4, P across all sts, break Stroll Sock yarn. 100 (109, 118, 127, 136, 145) sts.

Shape Raglan
Begin working in Garter st, using 2 strands of Alpaca Cloud.
Set Up Row 1 (RS): K all sts, decreasing 34 (37, 40, 43, 40, 49) sts evenly across. 66 (72, 78, 84, 96, 96) sts.
Row 2 (WS): K across all sts.

Begin Raglan Shaping
Raglan Shaping Row (RS): K2tog, K across to last 3 sts, SSK, K1. 2 sts dec.
Work Raglan Shaping Row every 4th row 7 (5, 5, 5, 2, 5) more times, then every RS row 17 (21, 23, 25, 33, 29) times. WE for 1.25".
Place remaining 16 (18, 20, 22, 24, 26) sts on holder for back neck.

Sleeves (make 2)
Using one strand of Stroll Sock and one strand of Alpaca Cloud, with smaller 16" circular needles loosely CO 64 (64, 64, 68, 68, 68) sts.
Work K2, P2 Rib flat for 2", ending with a RS row.
Switch to larger needles.
Dec Row (WS): P all sts, decreasing 8 (8, 8, 10, 10, 10) sts evenly across row. 56 (56, 56, 58, 58, 58) sts.
Set-up Row: K1 (1, 1, 2, 2, 2), PM (1), work row 1 of Plait Cable stitch across next 54 sts, PM(2), K 1 (1, 1, 2, 2, 2) sts.

Shape Sleeve
Sleeve Inc Row (RS): K1, M1R, work as established to last st, M1L, K1. 2 sts inc.
Work a Sleeve Inc Row every 10th row 5 (0, 0, 0, 0, 0) more times, then every 8th row 5 (6, 1, 0, 0, 0) times, then every 6th row 0 (7, 12, 10, 4, 0) times, then every 4th row 0 (0, 3, 8, 17, 24) times.
Upon completion of this section you will have worked the Sleeve Increase Row a total of 11 (14, 17, 19, 22, 25) times. 78 (84, 90, 96, 102, 108) sts.
WE in established pattern until piece measures 18" or desired length to underarm from CO edge, ending with a WS row.

Raglan Shaping
Row 1 (RS): BO 4, K all sts.
Row 2 (WS): BO 4, P all sts, cut Stroll Sock yarn. 70 (76, 82, 88, 94, 100) sts.
Begin working in Garter St, using 2 strands of Alpaca Cloud held together.
Set-up Row 1 (RS): K all sts, evenly decreasing 24 (26, 28, 30, 32, 34) sts across. 46 (50, 54, 58, 62, 66) sts.
Row 2 (WS): K across all sts.

Begin Raglan Shaping
Raglan Shaping Row (RS): K1, K2tog, K across to last 3 sts, SSK, K1. 2 sts dec.
Rep Raglan Shaping every 4th row 13 (12, 12, 11, 12, 13) more times, then every RS row 4 (7, 9, 12, 12, 13) times. Raglan Shaping Row done a total of 18 (20, 22, 24, 25, 27) times leaving 10 (10, 10, 10, 12, 12) sts. Slip these live sts to a holder.

Finishing
Weave in ends and block to schematic. Sew sleeve seams. Set in sleeves and sew.

Neck Band
Using smaller 16" circular needle and one strand of Stroll Sock and Alpaca Cloud held together for Neck Band, transfer 10 (10, 10, 10, 12, 12) held sts from right sleeve to needle, transfer 16 (18, 20, 22, 24, 26) held sts from back to needle, transfer 10 (10. 10. 10, 12, 12) sts from left sleeve to needle, PU and K 16 (18, 20, 22, 24, 26) sts from front neck, PM and join to work in the rnd. 52 (56, 60, 64, 72, 76) sts.
Set-up Rnd: K 10 (10, 10, 10, 12, 12), *K1, M1; rep from * a total of 16 (18, 20, 22, 24, 26) times, K 10 (10, 10, 10, 12, 12), *K1, M1; rep from * a total of 16 (18, 20, 22, 24, 26) times, SM. 84 (92, 100, 108, 120, 128) sts.
Work K2, P2 Rib in the Rnd for 10 rows. BO loosely in pattern.

Weave in any remaining ends invisibly on the WS of fabric. Block Neck Band if desired.

Plait Cable Pattern (Flat)

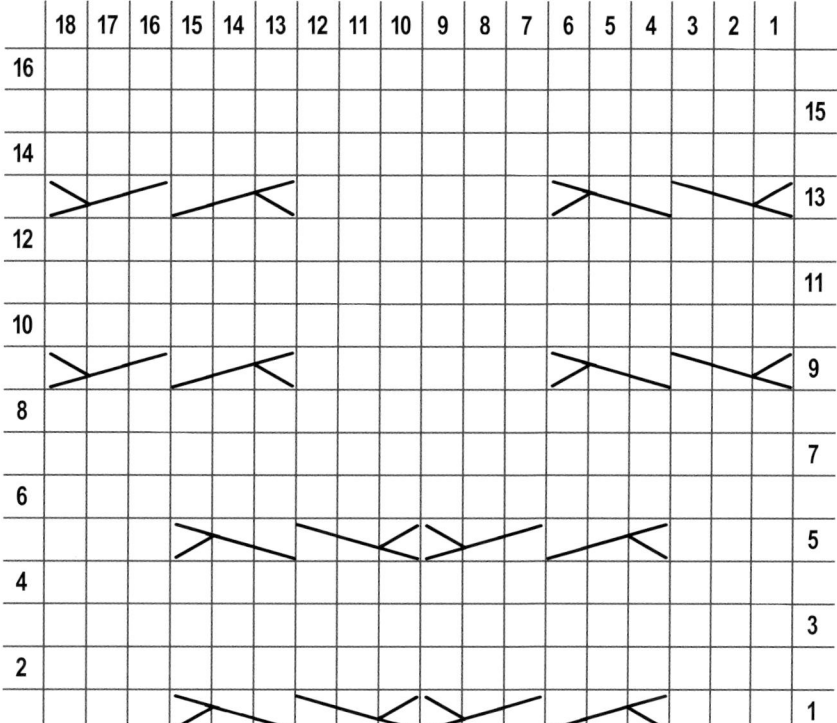

Legend

☐ K
RS: Knit stitch
WS: Purl stitch

C3 Over 3 Right (3/3 RC)
Sl3 to CN, hold in back. K3, K3 from CN.

C3 Over 3 Left (3/3 LC)
Sl3 to CN, hold in front. K3, K3 from CN.

Plait Cable Pattern (Circular)

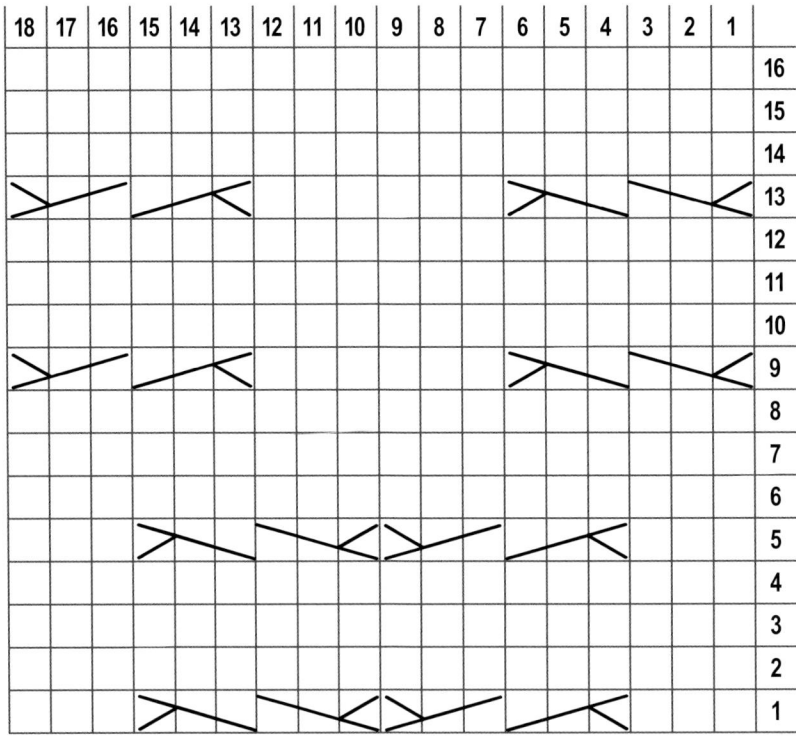

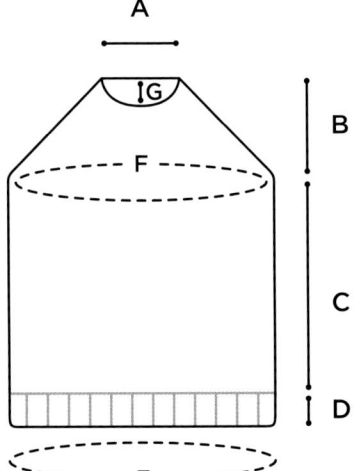

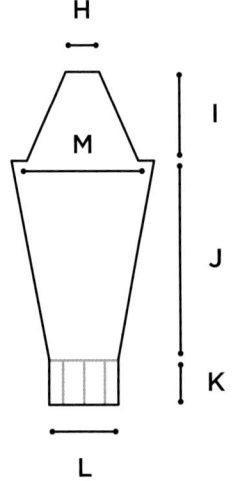

- A 12 (13.25, 14.25, 15.5, 17.25, 18.25)"
- B 8 (8, 8.5, 9, 9.5, 10)"
- C 13"
- D 2"
- E 36 (38.75, 41.75, 44.5, 48, 50.75)"
- F 36 (39, 42, 45, 48, 51)"
- G 1.25"
- H 2.5 (2.5, 2.5, 2.5, 3, 3)"
- I 8 (8.25, 8.75, 9, 9.5, 10)"
- J 16"
- K 2"
- L 8.75 (8.75, 8.75, 9.5, 9.5, 9.5)"
- M 12.75 (13.75, 14.75, 15.75, 16.75, 17.75)"

Note: Selvedge sts are not included in measurements

TWEEDY JUMPER

by Helen Metcalfe

FINISHED MEASUREMENTS
34.5 (38, 42, 45.5, 49.5, 53.5, 57, 61, 65)" finished bust measurement; garment is meant to be worn with 4" of ease.

YARN
Knit Picks Provincial Tweed (80% Superwash Fine Highland Wool, 20% Donegal Tweed; 250 yards/100g): Frozen Pond 27577, 4 (5, 6, 6, 7, 8, 9, 10, 11) skeins.

NEEDLES
US 7 (4.5mm) straight or circular needles plus DPNs or 16" circular needle for neckband, or one size smaller than size to obtain gauge.

US 8 (5mm) straight or circular needles, or size to obtain gauge.

NOTIONS
Yarn Needle
Stitch Marker
Cable Needle
Stitch Holder

GAUGE
21 sts and 24 rows = 4" over Main Cable Rep, blocked.

17 sts and 24 rows = 4" in St st, blocked.

Front Cable Panel = 11.75" wide.

For pattern support, contact hmetcalfe@hotmail.co.uk

Notes:
The front cable panel takes center stage here with a complimentary rib/cable pattern adorning the rest of the body. The jumper is worked in four separate pieces from the bottom up, seamed, with the neckband worked in the round.

Follow the charts from right to left on RS rows (odd numbers) and left to right on WS rows (even numbers).

C2 Over 2 Right (2/2 RC): Place 2 sts on CN and hold at back of work, K2 from LH needle then K2 from CN.
C2 Over 2 Left (2/2 LC): Place 2 sts on CN and hold at front of work, K2 from LH needle then K2 from CN.
C2 Over 2 Right P (2/2 RPC): Place 2 sts on CN and hold at back of work, K2 from LH needle then P2 from CN.
C2 Over 2 Left P (2/2 LPC): Place 2 sts on CN and hold at front of work, P2 from LH needle then K2 from CN.

Front Cable Panel (worked flat over 74 sts)
Row 1 (RS): P2, K4, *(P2, K2) x 4, P2, K4; rep from * twice more, P2.
Row 2 (WS): K2, *P4, (K2, P2) x 4, K2; rep from * twice more, P4, K2.
Row 3: P2, 2/2 LC, *(P2, K2) x 2, 2/2 RC, P2, K2, P2, 2/2 LC; rep from * twice more, P2.
Row 4: K2, *P4, K2, P2, K2, P6, K2, P2, K2; rep from * twice more, P4, K2.
Row 5: P2, K4, *P2, K2, P2, 2/2 RC, (K2, P2) x 2, K4; rep from * twice more, P2.
Row 6: Rep Row 4.
Row 7: P2, 2/2 LC, *P2, K2, 2/2 RC x 2, P2, K2, P2, 2/2 LC; rep from * twice more, P2.
Row 8: K2, *P4, K2, P2, K2, P10, K2; rep from * twice more, P4, K2.
Row 9: P2, K4, *P2, 2/2 RC x 2, (K2, P2) x 2, K4; rep from * twice more P2.
Row 10: Rep Row 8.
Row 11: P2, 2/2 LC, *2/2 RC, 2/2 RPC, K2, 2/2 LC, K2, P2, 2/2 LC; rep from * twice more, P2.
Row 12: K2, P4, *K2, P8, K2, P10; rep from * twice more, K2.
Row 13: 2/2 RPC, 2/2 LPC, *2/2 LC, P2, 2/2 LPC, 2/2 LC, 2/2 RPC, 2/2 LPC; rep from * twice more.
Row 14: P2, *K4, P8, K4, P6; rep from * twice more, K4, P2.
Row 15: K2, P4, * 2/2 LC x 2, P2, 2/2 LPC, 2/2 LC, P4; rep from * twice more, K2.
Row 16: P2, *K4, P6, K4, P8; rep from * twice more K4, P2.
Row 17: 2/2 LPC, 2/2 RPC, *2/2 LC x 2, P2, 2/2 LC x 2, 2/2 RPC; rep from * twice more.
Row 18: K2, *P10, K2, P8, K2; rep from * twice more, P4, K2.
Row 19: P2, 2/2 LC, *P2, K2, 2/2 LPC, K2, 2/2 RC, 2/2 RPC, 2/2 LC; rep from * twice more, P2.
Row 20: K2, *P4, K2, P10, K2, P2, K2; rep from * twice more, P4, K2.
Row 21: P2, K4, *(P2, K2) x 2, 2/2 RC x 2, P2, K4; rep from * twice more, P2.
Row 22: Rep Row 20.
Row 23: P2, 2/2 LC, *P2, K2, P2, 2/2 RC, 2/2 RPC, K2, P2, 2/2 LC; rep from * twice more, P2.
Row 24: Rep Row 4.
Row 25: P2, K4, *(P2, K2) x 2, 2/2 RC, P2, K2, P2, K4; rep from * twice more, P2.
Row 26: Rep Row 4.
Row 27: P2, 2/2 LC, *P2, K2, P2, 2/2 RPC, (K2, P2) x 2, 2/2 LC; rep from * twice more, P2.
Row 28: Rep Row 2.
Rep Rows 1-28 for pattern.

Main Cable Rep (worked flat over a multiple of 10 sts)
Row 1 (RS): P2, K4, P2, K2.
Row 2 (WS): P2, K2, P4, K2.
Row 3: P2, 2/2 RC, P2, K2.
Row 4: Rep Row 2.
Rep Rows 1-4 for pattern.

DIRECTIONS

Back
The back is worked flat from the bottom up.
Using smaller needles CO 92 (102, 112, 122, 132, 142, 152. 162, 172) sts.
Row 1: K2, *P1, K1; rep from * to end.
Row 2: *P1, K1; rep from * to last 2 sts, P2.
Rep the last 2 rows a further 4 times.
Change to larger needles.
Row 1: Rep written or chart instructions for Main Cable Rep Row 1 until last 2 sts, P2.
Row 2: K2, rep written or chart instructions for Main Cable Rep Row 2 to end.
Rows 1-2 set the position of Main Cable Rep for the entirety of the back piece. Cont to rep Main Cable Rep until piece measures 18.25 (18.25, 18.25, 18, 18, 17.25, 16.75, 16.75, 16.5)" or desired length to underarm, ending after a WS row.

Armhole shaping
Maintaining pattern BO 2 (3, 3, 4, 5, 5, 6, 6, 6) sts at the beginning of the next 2 rows. 88 (96, 106, 114, 122, 132, 140, 150, 160) sts.
Maintaining pattern BO - (2, 2, 3, 4, 4, 5, 5, 5) sts at the beginning of the next - (2, 2, 2, 2, 2, 2, 2, 2) rows. - (92, 102, 108, 114, 124, 130, 140, 150) sts.
Maintaining pattern BO - (-, -, 2, 3, 3, 4, 4, 4) sts at the beginning of the next - (-, -, 2, 2, 2, 2, 2, 2) rows. - (-, -, 104, 108, 118, 122, 132, 142) sts.
Maintaining pattern BO - (-, -, -, 2, 2, 3, 3, 3) sts at the beginning of the next - (-, -, -, 2, 2, 2, 2, 2) rows. - (-, -, -, 104, 114, 116, 126, 136) sts.

Maintaining pattern BO - (-, -, -, -, -, 2, 2, 2) sts at the beginning of the next - (-, -, -, -, -, 2, 2, 2) rows. - (-, -, -, -, -, 112, 122, 132) sts

Dec Row (RS): P1, P2tog TBL, maintain pattern to last 3 sts, P2tog, P1. 2 sts dec.

Rep the Dec Row every RS row a further 2 (2, 5, 3, 2, 5, 4, 8, 13) times. 82 (86, 90, 96, 98, 102, 102, 104, 104) sts.

Maintaining pattern, cont without shaping until piece measures 25.25 (25.5, 26.25, 26.5, 26.75, 26.75, 26.75, 27.25, 27.5)" from bottom edge, ending after a WS row.

Shoulder Shaping

Maintain pattern throughout shoulder shaping.
BO 6 (6, 6, 7, 7, 7, 7, 8, 8) sts at the beginning of the next 2 rows. 70 (74, 78, 82, 84, 88, 88, 88, 88) sts.
BO 5 (6, 6, 6, 7, 7, 7, 7, 7) sts at the beginning of the next 2 rows. 60 (62, 66, 70, 70, 74, 74, 74, 74) sts.
BO 5 (5, 6, 6, 6, 7, 7, 7, 7) sts at the beginning of the next 2 rows. 50 (52, 54, 58, 58, 60, 60, 60, 60) sts
Place remaining sts on a st holder.

Front

The front is worked flat from the bottom up.

Hem

Using smaller needles CO 92 (102, 112, 122, 132, 142, 152, 162, 172) sts.
Row 1: K2, *P1, K1; rep from * to end.
Row 2: *P1, K1; rep from * to last 2 sts, P2.
Rep the last 2 rows a further 3 times.
Next Row: Rep Row 1.
Next Row: Rib 8 (6, 6, 6, 12, 10, 10, 10, 9) sts, *M1, rib 7 (8, 9, 10, 10, 11, 12, 13, 14) sts; rep from * 12 (12, 11, 11, 12, 12, 11, 11, 11) times, M- (-, 1, 1, -, -, 1, 1, 1), rib remaining - (-, 7, 6, -, -, 10, 9, 9) sts. 104 (114, 124, 134, 144, 154, 164, 174, 184) sts.
Change to larger needles.

Establish Pattern Placement

Row 1: P1 (6, 1, 6, 1, 6, 1, 6, 1), K2, rep written or chart instructions for Main Cable Rep Row one 1 (1, 2, 2, 3, 3, 4, 4, 5) times, P2, follow written or chart instructions for Front Cable Panel Row 23 (21, 19, 19, 17, 17, 17, 17, 15), P2, rep written or chart instructions for Main Cable Rep Row one 1 (1, 2, 2, 3, 3, 4, 4, 5) times, K2, P1 (6, 1, 6, 1, 6, 1, 6, 1).
Row 2: K1 (6, 1, 6, 1, 6, 1, 6, 1), P2, rep written or chart instructions for Main Cable Rep Row two 1 (1, 2, 2, 3, 3, 4, 4, 5) times, K2, follow written or chart instructions for Front Cable Panel Row 24 (22, 20, 20, 18, 18, 18, 18, 16), K2, rep written or chart instructions for Main Cable Rep Row two 1 (1, 2, 2, 3, 3, 4, 4, 5) times, P2, K1 (6, 1, 6, 1, 6, 1, 6, 1).
Rows 1-2 set the position of the cable sts for the entirety

of the front piece. Cont to follow chart or written st instructions until piece measures 18.25 (18.25, 18.25, 18, 18, 17.25, 16.75, 16.75, 16.5)" ending after a WS row.

Armhole Shaping

Cont to maintain pattern while working Armhole Shaping.

BO 2 (3, 3, 4, 5, 5, 6, 6, 6) sts at the beginning of the next 2 rows. 100 (108, 118, 126, 134, 144, 152, 162, 172) sts.

BO - (2, 2, 3, 4, 4, 5, 5, 5) sts at the beginning of the next - (2, 2, 2, 2, 2, 2, 2, 2) rows. - (104, 114, 120, 126, 136, 142, 152, 162) sts.

BO - (-, -, 2, 3, 3, 4, 4, 4) sts at the beginning of the next - (-, -, 2, 2, 2, 2, 2, 2) rows. - (-, -, 116, 120, 130, 134, 144, 154) sts.

BO - (-, -, -, 2, 2, 3, 3, 3) sts at the beginning of the next - (-, -, -, 2, 2, 2, 2, 2) rows. - (-, -, -, 116, 126, 128, 138, 148) sts.

BO - (-, -, -, -, -, 2, 2, 2) sts at the beginning of the next - (-, -, -, -, -, 2, 2, 2) rows. - (-, -, -, -, -, 124, 134, 144) sts.

Dec Row (RS): P1, P2tog TBL, maintain pattern to last 3 sts, P2tog, P1. 2 sts dec.

Rep the Dec Row every RS row a further 2 (2, 5, 3, 2, 5, 4, 8, 13) times. 94 (98, 102, 108, 110, 114, 114, 116, 116) sts. Maintaining pattern continue without shaping until piece measures 22.25 (22.5, 23.25, 23.5, 23.75, 23.75, 23.75, 24.25, 24.5)" from bottom edge ending after a WS row.

Left Front Neckline Shaping

Next Row (RS): Maintain pattern for 31 (33, 34, 36, 37, 39, 39, 40, 40) sts, turn, working these sts only, leaving remaining 63 (65, 68, 72, 73, 75, 75, 76, 76) sts on hold.

Next Row (WS): BO 5 sts, maintain pattern to end. 26 (28, 29, 31, 32, 34, 34, 35, 35) sts.

All RS rows unless otherwise stated: Maintain pattern.

Next WS Row: BO 4 sts, maintain pattern to end. 22 (24, 25, 27, 28, 30, 30, 31, 31) sts.

Next WS Row: BO 3 sts, maintain pattern to end. 19 (21, 22, 24, 25, 27, 27, 28, 28) sts.

Next WS Row: BO 2 sts, maintain pattern to end. 17 (19, 20, 22, 23, 25, 25, 26, 26) sts.

Dec Row (RS): Maintain pattern to last 3 sts, K2tog, K1. 1 st dec.

Maintaining pattern on WS rows, rep the Dec Row every RS row a further - (1, 1, 2, 2, 3, 3, 3, 3) times. 16 (17, 18, 19, 20, 21, 21, 22, 22) sts.

Maintaining pattern continue without shaping until piece measures 25.25 (25.5, 26.25, 26.5, 26.75, 26.75, 26.75, 27.25, 27.5)" from bottom edge ending after a WS row.

Left Front Shoulder Shaping

Next Row (RS): BO 6 (6, 6, 7, 7, 7, 7, 8, 8) sts, maintain pattern to end. 10 (11, 12, 12, 13, 14, 14, 14, 14) sts.

Next Row (WS): Maintain pattern.

Next Row (RS): BO 5 (6, 6, 6, 7, 7, 7, 7, 7) sts, maintain pattern to end. 5 (5, 6, 6, 6, 7, 7, 7, 7) sts.

Next Row (WS): Maintain pattern.
Next Row: BO remaining sts.

Right Front Neckline Shaping
With RS facing rejoin yarn to 63 (65, 68, 72, 73, 75, 75, 76, 76) sts on hold. BO 32 (32, 34, 36, 36, 36, 36, 36, 36) sts, maintain pattern to end. 31 (33, 34, 36, 37, 39, 39, 40, 40) sts.
All WS rows unless otherwise stated: Maintain pattern.
Next Row (RS): BO 5 sts, maintain pattern to end. 26 (28, 29, 31, 32, 34, 34, 35, 35) sts.
Next RS Row: BO 4 sts, maintain pattern to end. 22 (24, 25, 27, 28, 30, 30, 31, 31) sts.
Next RS Row: BO 3 sts, maintain pattern to end. 19 (21, 22, 24, 25, 27, 27, 28, 28) sts.
Next RS Row: BO 2 sts, maintain pattern to end. 17 (19, 20, 22, 23, 25, 25, 26, 26) sts.
Next RS Row: K1, SSK, maintain pattern to end. 1 st dec. Maintaining pattern on WS rows, rep the last row every RS row a further - (1, 1, 2, 2, 3, 3, 3, 3) times. 16 (17, 18, 19, 20, 21, 21, 22, 22) sts.
Maintaining pattern continue without shaping until piece measures 25.25 (25.5, 26.25, 26.5, 26.75, 26.75, 26.75, 27.25, 27.5)" from bottom edge ending after a WS row.

Right Front Shoulder Shaping
Next Row (RS): Maintain pattern.
Next Row (WS): BO 6 (6, 6, 7, 7, 7, 7, 8, 8) sts, maintain pattern to end. 10 (11, 12, 12, 13, 14, 14, 14, 14) sts.
Next Row (RS): Maintain pattern.
Next Row (WS): BO 5 (6, 6, 6, 7, 7, 7, 7, 7) sts, maintain pattern to end. 5 (5, 6, 6, 6, 7, 7, 7, 7) sts.
Next Row (RS): Maintain pattern.
Next Row: BO remaining sts.

Sleeves
The sleeves are worked flat from the wrists up. Incorporate increased sts into Main Cable Rep pattern, but keep a border of at least 2 purl sts at all times to maintain a neat selvedge.
Using smaller needles CO 46 (50, 50, 54, 60, 60, 60, 62, 62) sts.
Row 1 (RS): K2, *P1, K1; rep from * to end.
Row 2 (WS): *P1, K1; rep from * to last 2 sts, P2.
Rep the last 2 rows a further 4 times.
Change to larger needles.
Row 1: P2 (4, 4, 1, 4, 4, 4, -, -), K2 (2, 2, -, 2, 2, 2, -, -), rep written or chart instructions for Main Cable Rep Row 1 until last 2 (4, 4, 3, 4, 4, 4, 2, 2) sts, P to end.
Row 2: K2 (4, 4, 3, 4, 4, 4, 2, 2) sts, rep written or chart instructions for Main Cable Rep Row 2 until last 4 (6, 6, 1, 6, 6, 6, 0, 0) sts, P2 (2, 2, -, 2, 2, 2, -, -), K2 (4, 4, 1, 4, 4, 4, -, -).
Inc Row: P2, M1, maintain pattern to last 2 sts, M1, P2. 2 sts inc.

While maintaining pattern, rep the Inc Row every 12 (12, 10, 10, 10, 10, 6, 4, 4) rows, followed by every - (14, 12, 12, -, -, -, 6, -) alternate rows, until there are 64 (66, 70, 74, 82, 82, 98, 108, 116) sts. Continue without shaping until piece measures 19.5 (19.5, 20.5, 20.5, 20.5, 20.5, 21.5, 21.5, 21.5)" from CO edge.

Top Arm Shaping
Maintaining pattern BO 2 (3, 3, 4, 5, 5, 6, 6, 6) sts at the beginning of the next 2 rows. 60 (60, 64, 66, 72, 72, 86, 96, 104) sts.
Decrease rows are worked as follows, please review instructions for your size as to how often these are worked over the coming section.
RS Dec Row: P1, SSP, maintain pattern to end, P2tog, P1. 2 sts dec.
WS Dec Row: K1, SSK, maintain pattern to end, K2tog, K1. 2 sts dec.

Sizes 34.5 (38, 42, 45.5, 49.5, 53.5, 57, -, -)"Only
Rep RS Dec Row 12 (13, 15, 16, 17, 17, 18, -, -) times, at the same time rep WS Dec Row every 2 (3, 5, 5, 4, 4, 2, -, -) WS rows 5 (4, 3, 3, 4, 4, 8, -, -) times. 26 (26, 28, 28, 30, 30, 34, -, -) sts.

Sizes 61, 65" Only
Rep RS Dec Row - (-, -, -, -, -, -, 19, 19) times, at the same time rep WS Dec Row every WS row - (-, -, -, -, -, -, 11, 14) times. - (-, -, -, -, -, -, 36, 38) sts.

All Sizes
Maintaining pattern BO 3 sts at the beginning of the next 2 rows. 20 (20, 22, 22, 24, 24, 28, 30, 32) sts.
Maintaining pattern BO 2 sts at the beginning of the next 2 rows. 16 (16, 18, 18, 20, 20, 24, 26, 28) sts.
BO remaining sts.

Neckband
Before completing neckband sew the shoulder seams.
With circular needle, RS facing, and starting at left front neck edge PU and K23 sts, PU and K28 (28, 30, 32, 32, 32, 32, 32, 32) sts from middle front bind off section, PU and K23 sts from right neck edge, K50 (52, 54, 58, 58, 60, 60, 60, 60) sts from back st holder. 124 (126, 130, 136, 136, 138, 138, 138, 138) sts. PM to mark beginning of rnd.
Next Rnd: *K1, P1; rep from * to end.
Rep the last rnd until neckband measures 1.5".
BO loosely.

Finishing
Line up the center of the sleeve cap with the shoulder seam, joining the seams using mattress st. Sew sleeve seams. Sew side seams. Weave in ends and block to schematic measurements.

Front Cable Pattern Chart

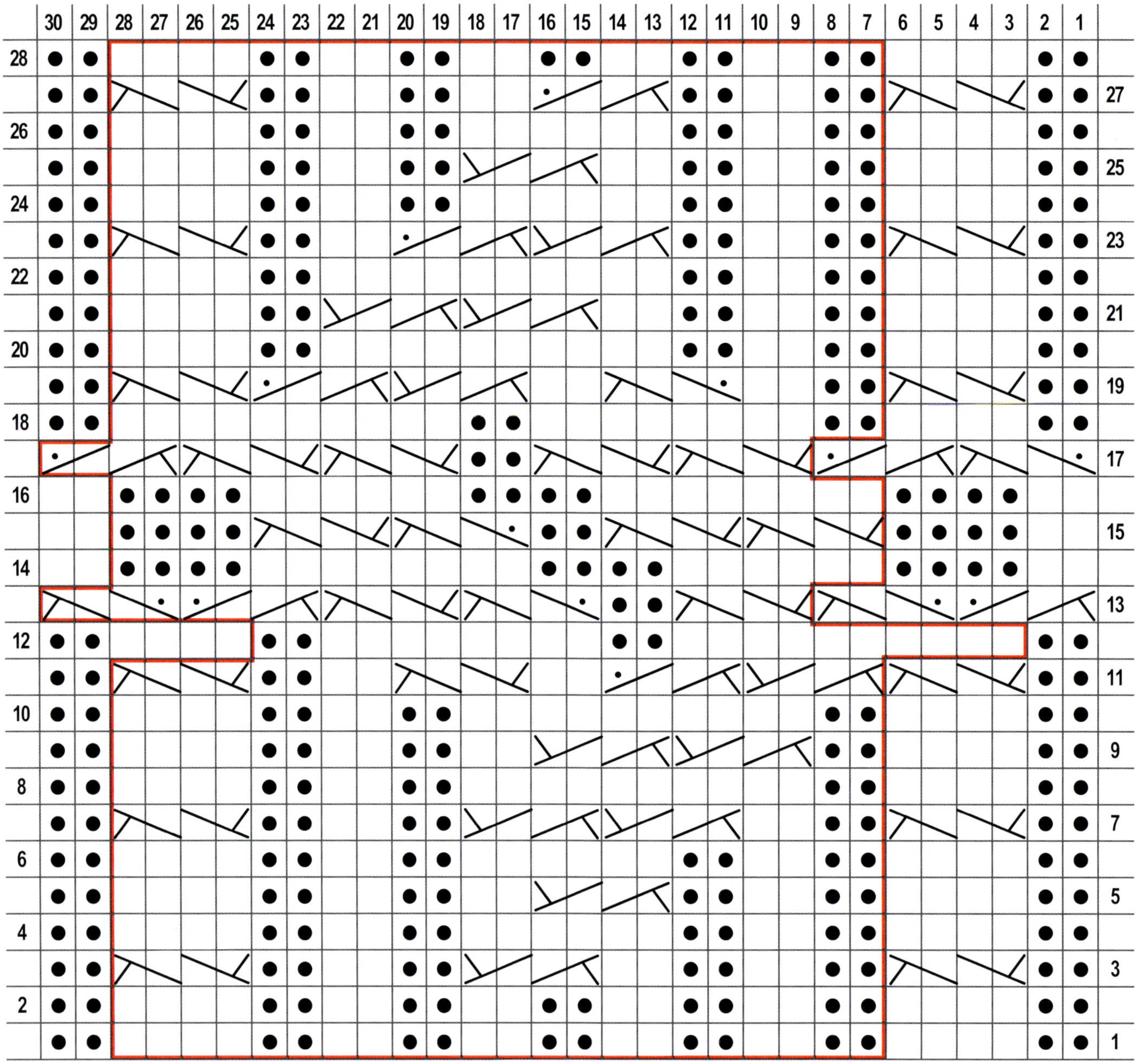

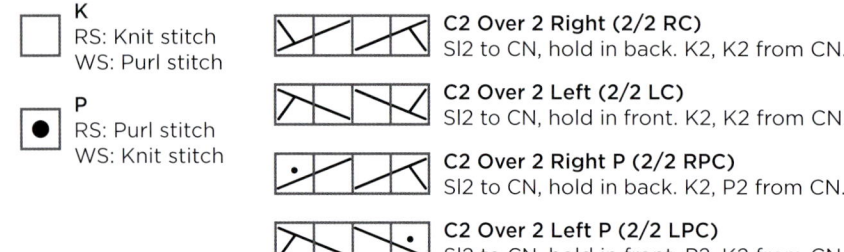

Legend

- **K** — RS: Knit stitch / WS: Purl stitch
- **P** — RS: Purl stitch / WS: Knit stitch
- **C2 Over 2 Right (2/2 RC)** — Sl2 to CN, hold in back. K2, K2 from CN.
- **C2 Over 2 Left (2/2 LC)** — Sl2 to CN, hold in front. K2, K2 from CN.
- **C2 Over 2 Right P (2/2 RPC)** — Sl2 to CN, hold in back. K2, P2 from CN.
- **C2 Over 2 Left P (2/2 LPC)** — Sl2 to CN, hold in front. P2, K2 from CN.

Main Cable Rep Chart

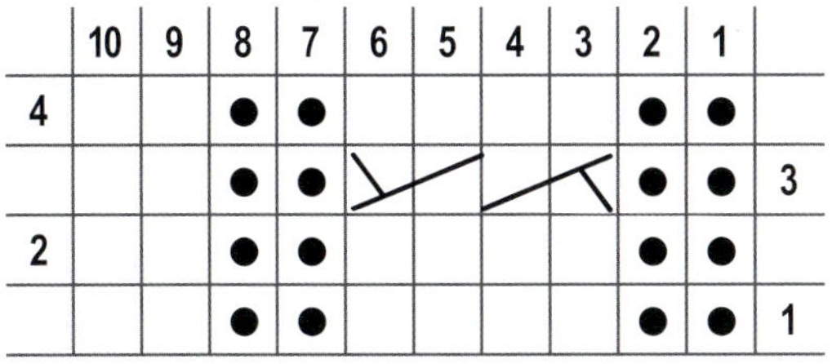

	10	9	8	7	6	5	4	3	2	1	
4			●	●					●	●	
			●	●	\			/	●	●	3
2			●	●					●	●	
			●	●					●	●	1

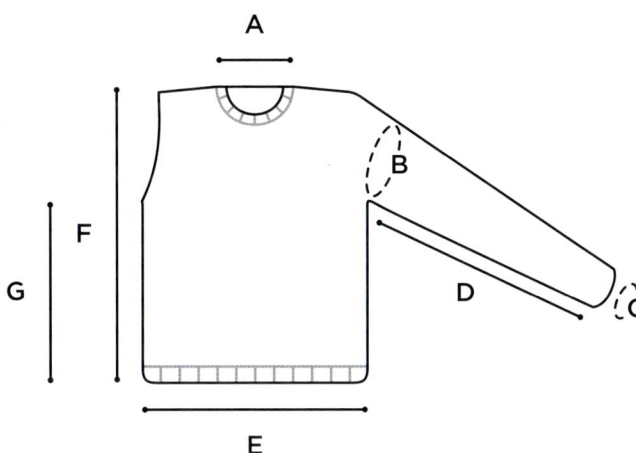

- **A** 17.25 (19, 21, 22.75, 24.75, 26.75, 28.5, 30.5, 32.5)"
- **B** 18.25 (18.25, 18.25, 18, 18, 17.25, 16.75, 16.75, 16.5)"
- **C** 26.25 (26.5, 27.25, 27.5, 27.75, 27.75, 27.75, 28.25, 28.5)"
- **D** 19.5 (19.5, 20.5, 20.5, 20.5, 20.5, 21.5, 21.5, 21.5)"
- **E** 8.5 (9.25, 9.25, 10, 11, 11, 11, 11.5, 11.5)"
- **F** 11.75 (12.25, 13, 13.75, 15.25, 15.25, 18.25, 20.25, 21.75)"
- **G** 9.5 (10, 10.25, 11, 11, 11.5, 11.5, 11.5, 11.5)"

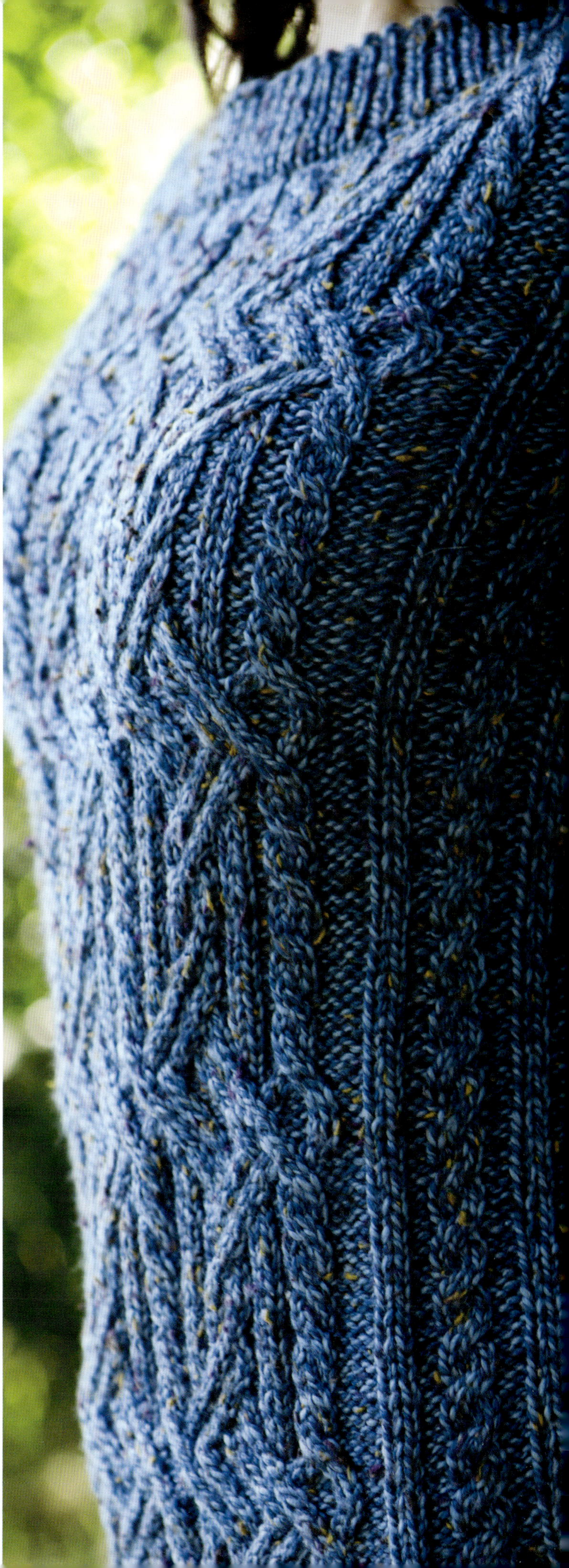

WOODSTOCK
by Sierra Morningstar

FINISHED MEASUREMENTS
33.5 (36.25, 39, 41.75, 44.5, 47.25, 50, 52.75, 55.75, 58.5, 61.25, 64)" finished bust measurement; garment is meant to be worn with 6-8" of ease.

YARN
Knit Picks Wool of the Andes
(100% Peruvian Highland Wool; 110 yards/50g): Claret Heather 24071, 11 (12, 12, 14, 14, 15, 16, 17, 18, 19, 19, 20) balls.

Knit Picks Alpaca Cloud Fingering
(100% Superfine Alpaca; 200 yards/50g): Oscar 26895, 6 (7, 7, 8, 8, 8, 9, 9, 10, 10, 11, 11) skeins.

NEEDLES
US 10 (6 mm) straight or circular needle, long enough to accommodate half of finished circumference, plus DPNs or 16" circular needle, or size to obtain gauge.

US 9 (5.5 mm) straight or circular needle, long enough to accommodate half or finished circumference, plus DPNs or 16" circular needles, or one size smaller than needle used to obtain gauge.

NOTIONS
Cable Needle
Scrap Yarn or Stitch Holders
Stitch Marker
Yarn Needle

GAUGE
23 sts and 27 rows = 4" in Honeycomb Cable pattern with a strand of each yarn held together on larger needles, blocked.

For pattern support, contact Morn5420@yahoo.com

Notes:

Woodstock is knit in pieces and seamed. One strand of Wool of the Andes and one strand of Alpaca Cloud are held together throughout.

The first and last stitch of each row is a selvedge stitch worked in St st, and is not included in the final measurements. When working the chart, read RS rows (odd numbers) from right to left, and WS rows (even numbers) from left to right.

C2 Over 2 Right (2/2 RC): Sl2 sts onto CN and hold in back, K2, K2 from CN.
C2 Over 2 Left (2/2 LC): Sl2 sts onto CN and hold in front, K2, K2 from CN.

Honeycomb Cable (worked flat over multiples of 8 sts)
Row 1 (RS): *2/2 RC, 2/2 LC; rep from * to end of row.
Row 2 and every WS Row through Row 8: Purl.
Row 3: Knit.
Row 5: *2/2 LC, 2/2 RC; rep from * to end of row.
Row 7: Knit.
Rep Rows 1-8 for pattern.

2x2 Rib (worked flat over multiples of 4 sts)
Row 1 (RS): *K2, P2; rep from * to end of row.
Row 2 (WS): *K2, P2; rep from * to end of row.
Rep Rows 1-2 for pattern.

2x2 Rib (worked in the rnd over multiples of 4 sts)
Rnd 1: *K2, P2; rep from * to end of rnd.
Rep Rnd 1 for pattern.

Stockinette Stitch (St st, work flat)
Row 1 (RS): Knit.
Row 2 (WS): Purl.
Rep Rows 1-2 for pattern.

DIRECTIONS

Hold one strand of each yarn together throughout pattern.

Back

With smaller needle, CO 98 (106, 114, 122, 130, 138, 146, 154, 162, 170, 178, 186) sts.

Work in 2x2 Rib with a 1 st St st selvedge on each end until piece measures 2" from CO edge, ending with a WS row. Change to larger needle.
Work in Honeycomb Cable Pattern maintaining St st selvedge until piece measures 22 (22, 22, 22, 22, 22, 23.25, 23.25, 23.25, 23.25, 23.25, 23.25)" from CO edge, ending with pattern Row 1 or 5.

Next Row (WS): P30 (34, 38, 38, 42, 46, 50, 54, 58, 58, 62, 66) sts. Turn work and BO these sts.
Place next 38 (38, 38, 46, 46, 46, 46, 46, 54, 54, 54) sts on holder for back neck.
With WS still facing, attach new yarn and purl to end.
Turn and BO these sts.

Front

Work as for back until piece measures 20 (20, 20, 20, 20, 20, 21.25, 21.25, 21.25, 21.25, 21.25, 21.25)" from CO edge, ending with pattern Row 1 or 5.

Right Front
Next Row (WS): P37 (41, 45, 49, 53, 57, 61, 65, 69, 69, 73, 77) sts. Turn.
Next Row (RS): BO 3 (3, 3, 4, 4, 4, 4, 4, 4, 3, 3, 3) sts then work to end. 34 (38, 42, 45, 49, 53, 57, 61, 65, 66, 70, 74) sts remain for Right Front.
Working the Right Front sts only, cont in pattern and BO at the beginning of the next 3 (3, 3, 3, 3, 3, 3, 3, 3, 4, 4, 4) RS rows as follows: 2 (2, 2, 3, 3, 3, 3, 3, 3, 3, 3, 3) sts, then 1 (1, 1, 2, 2, 2, 2, 2, 2, 2, 2, 2) st(s), then 1 (1, 1, 2, 2, 2, 2, 2, 2, 2, 2, 2) st(s), then - (-, -, -, -, -, -, -, -, 1, 1, 1) st(s). 30 (34, 38, 38, 42, 46, 50, 54, 58, 58, 62, 66) shoulder sts remain.
Work in pattern for 5 (5, 5, 5, 5, 5, 5, 5, 5, 3, 3, 3) rows more, ending with pattern Row 6 or 2.
BO shoulder sts.

Left Front
With WS facing, place next 24 (24, 24, 24, 24, 24, 24, 24, 32, 32, 32) sts on holder for neck. Attach yarn and purl to end.
Working the Left Front only, cont in pattern and BO at the beginning of the next 4 (4, 4, 4, 4, 4, 4, 4, 5, 5, 5) WS rows as follows: 3 (3, 3, 4, 4, 4, 4, 4, 3, 3, 3) sts, then 2 (2, 2, 3, 3, 3, 3, 3, 3, 3, 3) sts, then 1 (1, 1, 2, 2, 2, 2, 2, 2, 2, 2) st(s), then 1 (1, 1, 2, 2, 2, 2, 2, 2, 2, 2) st(s), then - (-, -, -, -, -, -, -, -, 1, 1, 1) st(s). 30 (34, 38, 38, 42, 46, 50, 54, 58, 58, 62, 66) shoulder sts remain.
Work in pattern for 4 (4, 4, 4, 4, 4, 4, 4, 4, 2, 2, 2) rows more, ending with pattern Row 6 or 2.
BO shoulder sts.

Sleeves (Make 2)

Sleeves are worked flat from the top down.
With larger needles CO 82 (82, 82, 90, 90, 98, 98, 98, 106, 106, 114, 114) sts.

Starting with WS Row 2, work in Honeycomb Cable Pattern with a 1 st St st selvedge on each end for 2 (2, 2, 2, 2, 1, 1, 1.5, 1.5, 1, 1, 1)", ending with a WS row.

Dec Row (RS): K1, SSK, K to last 3 sts, K2tog, K1. 2 sts dec. Cont in pattern and rep Dec Row every 6th row 7 (7, 7, 8, 8, 14, 14, 5, 12, 14, 7, 7) more times, every 8th row 4 (4, 4, 3, 3, -, -, 6, -, -, -, -) times, then every 4th row - (-, -, -, -, 1, 1, -, 3, 1, 12, 12) times. 58 (58, 58, 66, 66, 66, 66, 74, 74, 74, 74, 74) sts.

If there are not enough sts at the beginning and end of row to work a complete cable, work these sts in St st. WE until sleeve measures 14.5 (14.5, 14.5, 15, 15, 15, 15, 15.5, 15.5, 15.5, 16, 16)" or 2" shorter than desired length, ending with a pattern Row 1 or 5.

Change to smaller needle.
Beginning with a WS Row, work in 2x2 Rib with St st selvedge sts until cuff measures 2".
BO all sts.

Finishing

Weave in ends. Wash and block pieces to measurements.
Sew Front to Back at shoulders.
Sew sleeves to Body, making sure center of sleeve is at shoulder seam.
Beginning at bottom, seam side from hem to armhole, then seam sleeve from armhole to cuff.

Turtleneck

Place held front and back neck sts on spare needle.
With smaller circular needle or DPNs, starting at right back shoulder, PU 1 st.
Work across back neck sts as follows, K1, *P2, K2; rep from * to last st, P1. PU 13 (13, 13, 17, 17, 17, 17, 17, 17, 17, 17, 17) sts around left front neck, work held neck sts in 2x2 Rib starting with K2, PU 12 (12, 12, 16, 16, 16, 16, 16, 16, 16, 16, 16) sts around right front neck. 88 (88, 88, 104, 104, 104, 104, 104, 104, 120, 120, 120) sts.
PM and join for knitting in the rnd.
Work in 2x2 Rib for 3.5". Change to larger circular needle and continue in 2x2 Rib for an additional 3.5".
Bind off.
Fold turtleneck over to the outside, and tack in place if desired.

Honeycomb Cable Chart

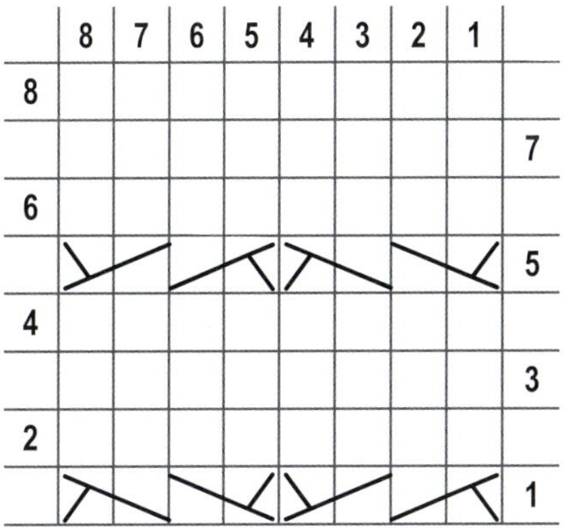

	8	7	6	5	4	3	2	1
8								
								7
6								
								5
4								
								3
2								
								1

Legend

☐ K
RS: Knit stitch
WS: Purl stitch

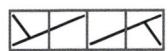
C2 Over 2 Right (2/2 RC)
Sl2 to CN, hold in back. K2, K2 from CN.

C2 Over 2 Left (2/2 LC)
Sl2 to CN, hold in front. K2, K2 from CN.

Abbreviations

BO	bind off	**KFB**	knit into the front and back of stitch	**PU**	pick up	**SSP**	sl, sl, p these 2 sts tog tbl
BOR	beginning of round	**K-wise**	knitwise	**P-wise**	purlwise	**SSSK**	sl, sl, sl, k these 3 sts tog
cn	cable needle	**LH**	left hand	**rep**	repeat	**St st**	stockinette stitch
CC	contrast color	**M**	marker	**Rev St st**	reverse stockinette stitch	**sts**	stitch(es)
CDD	Centered double dec	**M1**	make one stitch	**RH**	right hand	**TBL**	through back loop
CO	cast on	**M1L**	make one left-leaning stitch	**rnd(s)**	round(s)	**TFL**	through front loop
cont	continue	**M1R**	make one right-leaning stitch	**RS**	right side	**tog**	together
dec	decrease(es)	**MC**	main color	**Sk**	skip	**W&T**	wrap & turn (see specific instructions in pattern)
DPN(s)	double pointed needle(s)	**P**	purl	**Sk2p**	sl 1, k2tog, pass slipped stitch over k2tog: 2 sts dec		
EOR	every other row	**P2tog**	purl 2 sts together	**SKP**	sl, k, psso: 1 st dec	**WE**	work even
inc	increase	**PM**	place marker	**SL**	slip	**WS**	wrong side
K	knit	**PFB**	purl into the front and back of stitch	**SM**	slip marker	**WYIB**	with yarn in back
K2tog	knit two sts together	**PSSO**	pass slipped stitch over	**SSK**	sl, sl, k these 2 sts tog	**WYIF**	with yarn in front
						YO	yarn over

Knit Picks yarn is both luxe and affordable—a seeming contradiction trounced! But it's not just about the pretty colors; we also care deeply about fiber quality and fair labor practices, leaving you with a gorgeously reliable product you'll turn to time and time again.

THIS COLLECTION FEATURES

Stroll Sock Yarn
Fingering Weight
75% Fine Superwash Merino Wool, 25% Nylon

Swish
Worsted Weight
100% Fine Superwash Merino Wool

Paragon
Sport Weight
50% Fine Merino, 25% Baby Alpaca, 25% Mulberry Silk

Wool of the Andes
Worsted Weight
100% Peruvian Highland Wool

Gloss
DK Weight
70% Merino Wool, 30% Silk

Simply Wool
Worsted Weight
100% Eco Wool

Alpaca Cloud
Fingering Weight
100% Superfine Alpaca

Provincial Tweed
Worsted Weight
80% Superwash Fine Highland Wool, 20% Donegal Tweed

View these beautiful yarns and more at www.KnitPicks.com